CORNELIU LEU

Roosevelt, Churchill, Stalin and Hitler – their surprising role in Eastern Europe in 1944

Editor: Michael M. Dediu
United States of America

DERC Publishing House
Tewksbury (Boston), Massachusetts, U. S. A.

Copyright ©2013 by Corneliu Leu

All rights reserved

Published and printed in the
United States of America

Library of Congress Cataloging in Publication Data

Corneliu Leu

Roosevelt, Churchill, Stalin and Hitler – their surprising role in Eastern Europe in 1944

ISBN-13: 978-1-939757081

A FASCINATING STORY OF THE EXPLOSIVE EVENTS DURING WORLD WAR II IN ROMANIA

A NEW VERSION OF

CORNELIU LEU'S

THE NOVEL OF A GREAT DAY

BASED ON HISTORICAL DOCUMENTS,

NEWSPAPERS PUBLISHED AT THAT TIME,

DIPLOMATIC MAIL AND REPORTS

AND AUTHOR'S INTERVIEWS WITH PARTICIPANTS AT THOSE EVENTS

This book is a abridgment of the complete editions entitled „Romanul unei zile mari" printed in 1979, 1984 and 1989 by the „Albatros" Publishing House.

4   Roosevelt, Churchill, Stalin and Hitler – their surprising role in Eastern Europe in 1944

Editor's Note

With over 65 years of intense and successful literary activity, Corneliu Leu has a well established reputation. This book brings a shiny light on the mysterious and little known events from the World War II in Eastern Europe, where Roosevelt, Churchill, Stalin and Hitler had astonishing influence and interests.

Based on numerous historical documents, and on interviews with important people involved in those tumultuous events, the author brings to life, with a remarkable talent, the vibrant atmosphere of those very difficult times.

This is a book which will delight all the readers who like history presented in an exquisite literary style, and who want to discover many unknown details from the world's boisterous past.

Michael M. Dediu
U. S. A.

6 Roosevelt, Churchill, Stalin and Hitler – their surprising role in Eastern Europe in 1944

I. MADNESS AND PRAGMATISM AT RASTENBURG

The pomp of former times has disappeared from Hitler's headquarters. The atmosphere is charged, full - of suspense and an almost conspiratorial silence in which measures of precaution and defense have taken the place of protocol. The manner in which you are greeted, the manner in which you are accompanied along the corridors, the silence in which you remain and wait, everything suggests a cold tension, menacing and menaced at the same time.

In the chamber of concrete which enhances the gray silence to an even greater extent, Antonescu turns towards his assistants. He feels the urge to comment on the changes that have occurred. But he renounces. His military, upbringing has taught him to speak only to give orders and not to comment.

He endeavors to look calm, to inject his companions with confidence and to rouse on the part of the Führer's men the respect which has, always been his due.

It is, however, rather difficult for him to make-believe and his abrupt, harsh. gestures somewhat betray the anxiety besetting him.

Through the window, you can see a part of the entrance to the shelter, the shell-proof bunker. And hard by, like a helpless grin, stands the mined wall of the hut in which, only fifteen days earlier, the attempt on Hitler's life took place.

Indeed, like a grin which seems to be answering the Romanian Marshal's hidden thoughts: "You shan't succeed, you shan't succeed, you shan't succeed!..."

Angry, abruptly changing the position of his small body, Antonescu tries to turn away not only his eyes but his entire being from that image which now he finds either laughable or mocking. Because his own voice, of two weeks ago, echoes in his mind.

It was July the 20th; he was told that Hitler had survived-an attempt upon his life undertaken by a group of generals, and he said spitefully: He'd better be dead...

"He'd better be dead"; "He'd better be dead"; "He'd better be dead"... Against his will he can hear his voice-resounding in the narrow corridors at Rastenburg. A shrill voice, giving away his thoughts, putting guards on the alert, mixing with, the tramp of boots and with the sinister grin of the ruins he could see out of the window and which seemed to be making a mock of him. "Well, it is not over with him; Hitler is alive".

The Marshal forces himself to check his thoughts, to forget his own voice and what he had then said. But he can't do it and although he has turned his eyes away from the window overlooking the ruins, he keeps seeing their hideous grinning mouth.

And it seems to him that the words he had uttered then resound ever louder here, in Hitler's bunker, as if anyone recorded them on tape and now played them back. As a proof that his words have met Hitler's ear and the punishment will come today.

The punishment?... For a long time now, in his nightmares, the Marshal has dreamt that he was caught, detained somewhere, without any possibility to react. He has dreamt of upright walls, just like the walls of the bunker, slippery metal walls which he cannot even cling to.

Indeed, his thoughts almost convince him that he has been summoned to Hitler's presence in order to be arrested. At best, he will be retained as a hostage, as Horthy in 1943, when Kallay attempted a coup d'état in Hungary and Hitler summoned Horthy to him, too.

Hostage!... He glances at the tall, narrow walls which look old, but about which it is difficult to tell whether they belong to the old fortress or to the impugnable shelter, and he is convinced that he will never emerge from their confinement.

Slowly turning his tormented effigy-like head, red with the tension and the reflexes of his thin hair, the Marshal seems to be surveying the assistants accompanying him, in order to establish which will be the first to betray him and which the first to deny him. His faded glance rests on, the handsome face, framed by black locks of hair, and endowed with fascinating long lashed eyes, of the man who has made the most solemn declaration of loyalty to him in his whole life - Mihai Antonescu. And, by an association of ideas, he recalls that Hitler is retaining Horia Sima somewhere nearby, that rebel iron-guardist as a threat, as a proof that he, Antonescu, could be replaced any time.

With a glint of severity in his glance the Marshal surveys his assistants faces anew and sees with his mind's eye the manner in which they will leave this shelter: submissive, bowing their head to their new chief commander, governor or whatever other assignment Hitler may entrust to him, while his own head, severed by the axe of some SS executioner, will tumble to the ground and roll over and over...

If only he had the will-power to hinder his body from writhing after his head has been severed! For he has heard, or has read somewhere that, after being beheaded, one's body writhes. Lacking reason it twitches and kicks in the same way as a beheaded bird tries to flap its wings. And that would be unusually degrading: that he, Marshal Antonescu, a man who would know how to die with dignity, should, against his will, come to die writhing like a beheaded cock. No, no, such a thing cannot be!... And, with a ridiculous ambition, he tries in his innermost self to build up wave upon wave of will-power to persuade himself now of the need to be dignified even in the situation in which he would be headless.

He is a short man, with a tense face, of commonplace maturity, on which the passage of time has not left many traces except for the thin red veins which congest it. His evil grey eyes are deep sunk in encircling pouches, while his chestnut brown hair, grey and short-cropped at the temples, is combed from one side to the other over the top of his head in order to cover his baldness. It is a mask-like face, and it is hard to tell how it looked in its youth and how it will look at old age. Moreover: it is hard to visualize how the Marshal would look dressed in either another uniform or as a civilian. In his tunic tailored after the English fashion, with trousers of a lighter tinge of color, tobacco-hued top-boots and a horsewhip which, in his ambitious gestures, acquires the virtues of a scepter, he is "the Marshal" and he can be conceived of only as an entity. His is a rather out-moded face, but it inspires respect. And it especially strikes with awe the German soldiery whose gland of discipline immediately begins to secret when encountering his authoritative presence.

And while he strides with growing dignity and proud profile, a dark thought keeps gnawing at his conscience: "It is too late, too late, too late; they were right to ask me to stop at the Dniester; now I have no choice: I must submit, and that to preserve the power of command in my country".

II

Hitler is not as mad as he is reported to be. On the contrary he is quite lucid, lugubruotisly so and he pursues his interests with the ability of a great strategist. It is only that he is in a state of extreme nervousness on account of the traces left by the bomb attempt on his mental condition and on his body by the wounds which still pain him.

He makes his appearance in a torpedo-like manner. When coming from the other basements, from the underground rooms of the precincts, a blast seems to precede him: With the nape of his neck and one of his hands bandaged, his fierce feline face acquires more expressivity when he feels pangs of pain shooting through his body due to the wounds received on the crown of his head.

Nobody dares to make the slightest gesture. But it is whispered that for some days now - a later impact of the shock - he has been suffering from equilibrium disorders.

The whispers reach Antonescu's ears, but he does not hear them. He records a certain degree of the tension emitted by the man approaching him. He feels how he is losing his self-control; he clenches his jaws in his own particular way, an action which lends his mien an evil expression of tension, and he hears the voice of his wife trying to hinder him from coming to this personal interview: "What if he has summoned you? Don't go! And if he orders you to be killed...?"

Therefore he does not hear the beginning of Hitler's sentence, and he is not aware whether the latter greeted him with words of welcome. All he hears is his question, which points to the fact that he is in no mood for retardation: "Herr Marshal, are you determined to fight alongside us to the end or not?!"

Antonescu grows even redder in the face: "Führer, your question is offensive!"

While hearing the echoes of his own voice he confronts Hitler's glance whereon he encounters the glitter of that malevolent lucidity with which he has always carried out his plans.

The latter attempting a motion with his bandaged hand, sets off an anguish of pain in his still fresh hurts and, all of a sudden, his body is seized with spasms. The giddiness which comes over him from time to time, not allowing him to forget about the bomb-plot commences again. He walks to and fro. A moan escapes his lips. He pushes forward his jaw, moustache and nose as if indistinctly wishing to bite. And seeking to conceal his crushing smarts of pain, he makes for one of the doors. Turning as if actuated by springs, his entire retinue follows him mechanically. But he, knowing his mind even in a situation of this kind, stops at the door and screams without ever turning his bandaged head round: "I'll be coming back! I'll be coming back ... Till then let them see the secret weapons!..."

"Let them see the secret weapons!"... "the secret weapons..." His shrill voice, reverberating resonantly against the underground concrete walls, hangs in the air like the sour smoke of an explosion sullying the Marshal's violet-blue cheeks which are full of large pores and cyanotic veins.

His small retinue, made up of four generals and three colonels, among whom Mihai Antonescu, wearing a black funerary suit, stands out, is stock still awaiting a gesture on his part. He is aware of this and so he attempts a motion.

The German officers who have remained in the chamber move around and with their disciplined solicitude ask whether they may let the screen come down. They receive no answer, for the guest's thoughts are elsewhere. Therefore, they let a white canvas descend mechanically against one of the walls while Ion Antonescu, dressed in his uniform of a Romanian marshal, with his initials written above the insignia of his epaulettes realizes that it is all over.

It is only now that it is all over. Till now, something still could have been done...

Indeed: why did he not curse Hitler?! Why did he not point out to him how indebted he was to him, how indebted he and all of Germany were to the Marshal!... Why did he not tell him that here and now, come what may, he was through with him. He is through with Hitler, come what may!... His body will not writhe after being beheaded. He is sure of that!...

But he did not tell him! Even when seized with spasms, Hitler knows how to dominate and he did dominate him!... With a bitter taste in his mouth, the Marshal sits down on a narrow straight chair, refusing the armchair which a young German officer offers him with a gesture of bewilderment.

He sits uncomfortably and bolts upright. His profile is lacking in expression, while the nape of his thin neck seems to be awaiting decapitation. His hair is reddish and thin, and it is come towards the left with the purpose of covering the baldness of his head whose shape is round enough to roll easily.

But apart from himself, nobody else is thinking about the nonsense which is from him. All of them, and particularly the hosts, attired in the defying uniforms of an army with a long-standing tradition are interested in his reactions of a great military specialist to the new weapons being shown on the screen.

Neither does Hitler suspect what thoughts are harassing his ally. In one of his favorite rooms, which looks like a boudoir or a family vault, he lies as if crucified in his bed while simultaneously receiving his injection and listening to the contents of a top-secret dossier which is being read to him by one of his secretaries. Suddenly, he withdraws his arm and looks ferociously at the third person in the chamber - the physician administering him the sedative. Then he screams at the secretary who is reading; with a mechanically disciplined monotony: "It's not to be done that way! You are reading all the secret reports to me? Read only the general data!"

The clean-shaven officer stares bemused at the long, typed pages. Another officer automatically takes over his place and begins to scan the pages of the dossier in an entirely different manner. He is specially trained to summarize. He takes in everything at one glance and articulates in a colorless, rather high-pitched voice, which seems to be purposely tuned at the position the standing at attention: "Ion Antonescu, Marshal of Romania, the head of the Romanian state. Born on..."

Hitler has ceased screaming. The effect of the sedative has seemingly begun to spread throughout his body. He lies with his closed eyes facing the ceiling, his moustache slightly twisted towards the left in a frozen rictus, as if he had died in that position... The voice of the reader, obviously standing at attention picks out the attributes from the long, sparsely typed pages: vegetarian, religious, honest, lacking property... megalomaniac - he deems himself to be the entitled leader of the Romanians, the one called upon to save them... He does not relish jokes, puns, witticisms; he compels his aides to employ a military language of formal relationship... He has no friends...

Something twitches in the Führer's death mask, as if a fly had disturbed his petrified repose. The officer reading the report senses it instinctively, clicks his heels and waits. The question comes: "What did you say?... Here, here towards the end..."

The heels click again and the voice repeats: "He does not relish jokes, puns, witticisms; he compels his aides..."

But the motionless body gives forth a shriek: "Not there!... Further on!"

Promptly, the officer raps out: "Military career: Cavalry Military School, cavalry officer in... captain in the 4th Army Corp; Chief of Bureau of Operations at General Staff Headquarters in Jazzy during the World War I, military attaché at the Romanian Legation in London immediately after the war... since 1924 the Commander of the 9th Cavalry Regiment, Brigadier General in the year..."

Hitler jumps to his feet and rasps nervously: "Faster, faster. Let me know immediately when the projection of the film is over. He begins to walk about the chamber feeling the walls as if wishing to convince himself of something, one by one he surveys the people around him while they shrink under his feverishly glance and, turning his ear to the officer who is reacting and rotating after him, he listens: "Chief of General Staff Headquarters from 1931 to 1935, disciplinarily transferred to the post of Division Commander at Pitesti, later on, being assigned a territorial command, he hands in his resignation which is not accepted... Minister of War in the Goga-Cuza government ... in 1939 he is appointed Commander of the Army Corps at Kishinev where his assignment is withdrawn while he is placed under house arrest at the Bistritza Monastery.. . In September 1940 he is appointed President of the Council of Ministers... Political affinities: before becoming Head of State he was drawn to the iron-guards movement... Attitude towards the royal family: in 1916 he does not grant leave of presence from the barracks to Mr Romalo, whom his friend, Prince Charles, had invited to tea. While Chief of General Staff Headquarters in 1934-1935, he declines to receive a stock of weapons jointly purchased abroad by the royal family and a number of politicians; at the same time he tutors down an invitation to a reception given by Mrs. Lupescu, the king's mistress, saying that he could not accept to go to a concubine together with his wife...   Published works: "The Romanians, Their Origin, Their Past, Their Sacrifices and Rights - a historical-national memoir of nationalistic orientation published in 1919. He asserts in this work that "the League of Nations is a utopia"; Fire and Movement - the principal elements of battle course of lectures delivered at the Higher Military Ate, Addressed to the Romanians- a collection of articles and speeds in which he expounds his wish for dictatorship and his anticommunist theories... Private relations: extremely few he has no friends. He has a reduced camarilla; his assistants are disciplined and obedient in carrying out orders. He has dismissed a number of acknowledged experts pretexting their incapacity, others he has pensioned off. His most intimate collaborator - Mihail Antonescu. He does not take into account the fact that the latter has attempted betrayal several times... At present, under his leadership, the political situation in..."

On Hitler's curt: "That's enough!..." the voice automatically stops.

The Führer seems to be inspired. His tousled eyebrows and moustache again make him acquire the appearance of a vicious Tom-cat with feverish eyes.

He orders the doctor: "A strong stimulant! I must speak a lot!... A lot and convincingly!..."

And, to the horror of the latter, who has just given him a shot of sedative, he stretches out his arm with its perforated vein which looks like that of a drug-addict.

Then, doped, he paces resolutely along the underground corridors.

He is proud of himself. It shows by the way he swings his arms: with sweeping movements, even though pangs of; pain shoot through them from time to time. And while pacing forward he whispers to himself: "Of course!.. He is an important ally. Yes, he is..."

As has become habitual with him of late, the last words of his inner thoughts are uttered aloud, a sign of his worn-out nerves. The men accompanying him walk close on his heels, ready at any moment to agree with him.

With a furious gesture, Hitler throws open the door of the chamber where the projection of the film is still under way and as if it were a perfectly logical continuation of their discussion, he addresses Antonescu beginning with the middle of the sentence.

Is Hitler excited? Are dark thoughts tormenting him or is he dominated by the sober, vile attitude, satanically held back like a bundle of will-power, of this gaunt marshal, shorter in height than himself and with narrow shoulders and uniform tailored after the English fashion?... Yes, indeed, he was told, it was mentioned in the report read to him that Antonescu was a military attaché in London and that ever since he has worn clothes tailor red after the English fashion!

But he refrains. His bandaged head, the white dressings of which set off his black brush of a moustache to an ever greater extent, makes a sign requiring everybody to leave the charmer. He concentrates trying to feel if the stimulant has made its effect and has given him a state of well-being.

His moustache rises equally at both ends, like :t curtain at the theatre being drawn up by mechanical devices, and uncovers a smile of satisfaction. The Führer feels well, powerful, energetic and combative. There is no need any longer to convince himself that the injection has made its effect. No. there is not. He feels well, so all is well in Europe, too!

He looks at his collocutor with kindness and amused, he asks himself what was there about this man that could have impressed him so much. He is rather slim in body. The position of his hands and the protruding shoulder blades betray a state of weariness. The regular features of his face, with the forehead, now and mouth well-proportioned, point to his having been a common place person. With nervous and slightly wheezing breads, the Marshal keeps his lips parted in the manner of children suffering from polyposis. And the lower jaw which, in spite of the well-cut features of the face, has something churlish and rough about it, lending the face that expression, of bold and-silent malignity.

Yes, this man is his ally! One of the few allies that has remained... Hitler glances once again at his forehead, grown broader because of baldness, at the abrupt delimitation and contrast between the white and red hair, at the grey eyes and nondescript eyebrows.

His eyes ringed by black circles have as evil goggling took about them. Hitler touches the black circles round his own eyes. He is happy that the other man has such circles too, that his face also betrays the traces of sleepless nights and torment. And due to this fact he gazes at him with benevolence, as if urging hint to unveil as many of his weaknesses as possible, as if telling him with tenderness: "Yes, my dear Marshal, relax, let that jag of yours sag and let your breath wheeze for I also have this feeling of suffocating!... Yes, that's right! These are, human weaknesses which we cannot overcome. Only the crux, the crux is altogether different. Look, now, for instance, I am convinced that we shall save Europe!"

As usually, he has uttered the last words aloud; but does not seem to be surprised at his own weakness. He only seeks to receive approval and he looks towards Keitel, the only person who has not left the chamber apart from the translator. Then, encouraged by the old soldier's look, he confidently lays the palm of his hand on the large operation map and he tells Antonescu, in the manner of a person offering a gift: "First of all, I wish to inform our ally briefly about the 20 July incident..." He becomes persuasive and proclaims, entirely delighted with the idea which has dawned upon him: "This plot was an incident which I personally had been expecting for years!... Yes, yes, for years! . . . " Seeking to penetrate the grey eyes of his interlocutor, Hitler, from time to time, turns his gaze towards Keitel who, politely confirms his words as if he were sprinkling spices over a meal which is too greasy. And he expounds an entire theory on the heterogeneous constitution the German Wehrmacht had had for years blending within its ranks wholly trustworthy elements with a genuine Germanic and Prussian conception on the one hand and dangerously intellectualized groups with international democratic views, pacifist reactionaries who exulted at any approach made towards Russia on the other. Beginning with 1942, the representatives of this orientation had become more and more active and they had tried by all means and ways to poison the morale at the front. The crisis ensuing last year as an outcome of these realities had as a consequence the suspension from their functions of the Marshals Manstein and Kleist and the necessity of putting an end to the intolerable circumstances, particularly to those behind the front, by assigning to these units new loyal military commanders who act energetically. Yes, indeed energetically, the Führer reiterates attempting to gesticulate with his bandaged hand while letting a groan of anger drop from his lips. But it is difficult to tel whether his anger is roused by the pain or by the words he is to pronounce now: The catastrophe at the Army Group "Centre"; called Mitte Group, was brought about this year by treacherous officers from the various headquarters and also by the action of their accomplices who held top key positions. But he, the Führer, is firmly confident that under a more effective command both their positions at the Dnieper and in the Crimea, as well as the front at Leningrad could have been held. What, does he not believe that?... The Marshal does not believe? His mien... Hitler spits the words out while persuasively inspecting his interlocutors eyes wherein there seems to persist a concealed mistrust. . . "He judges me solely as a member of a General Staff", Hitler reasons to himself as he recalls the data mentioned in the file previously read to him. A hint of suspicion steals into his face: "I wonder what Antonescu. said about the plot?"

He is silent. The wrinkles round his eyes point to his being inquisitive or baffled or only puzzled in a moment of prostration. Again he sees in his mind's eye the explosion of 20 July. He feels the burns at his head and hands, he actually feels them, for they still hurt him, he sees that lieutenant general falling, his name was Schmundt it seems, and he also sees those two colonels ... no, only one, Borgman was among the traitors, the following day he ordered his name to be erased from the list of the gravely wounded, he also sees Jodl squeezing his wound, and Kortez, and Buhle, and Bodenschatz, and the admirals Voss and Putthammer; then he sees Göring rushing in and yelling in a husky voice: "My Führer, you are alive!..." and then, correcting himself immediately, "you couldn't have fallen! ..." Then he sees Mussolini, agitated, flabby and idiotic.

With a blood-thirsty glare he shrieks: "The officers who took part in the criminal plot will be treated as perpetrators of criminal offence and, if they have not been killed by the troops who hate them, they will be brought before the Court Martial! They shall not be shot, they shall be hanged. " And then, on second thought, he specifies: "No, no; no trials will be staged. The

Wehrmacht will simply be cleansed ruthlessly and it will be oriented towards the high mission the German state has entrusted it with! Yes, there are always categorical solutions for carrying this out." Everything is cut and dry in the Führer's mind. The crisis that has recently occurred through the collapse of the middle sector of the eastern front - collapse brought about by the persons mentioned above – will be overcome! He regards the two generals with pride: "We will form 40 new divisions and brigades with the effective strength of divisions! Does Antonescu know what that means? It is terrific, it means a sure recovery. A sure one !" he yells on noticing the Marshal's desire to scan Keitel's countenance in order to find out if he, as an experienced soldier, believes Hitler's words. "Yes, it is," he ejaculates as if wishing to attract his glance and attention. "Today we have already formed a front which is being consolidated from hour to hour. The connection between the Army Group "Centre" and the northern army will be established and within at most four weeks - mark my words, Marshal! - the entire front will have been put into order again!. . ." But he has another solution too. A solution which anyone will understand to be a redeeming one. He will eliminate the sedentary part and he, the Führer of the Reich, will become the Commander in Chief of the Army inside the borders of the country ! On expounding his plan to the end, he grows calm. He seems to have forgotten about the spasms troubling him. For Hitler is conscious of the fact that, as long as his shrewd mind works properly, he will always find favorable solutions for Germany, he will devise formulas which Nazi thought will believe in.

IV

Antonescu is sad. A definite and discouraging sadness besets him, enveloping him in a feeling of impotence and futility.

Sadness. It is nothing but sadness. It is not fear, it is not the fear of death. It is sadness, generated by an unctuous feeling of embarrassment.

It is an almost suicidal sadness that has nothing whatsoever to do with the fear of death.

As if sensing him, with the receptive sensitivity characteristic of an agitated nervous system permanently alert,

Hitler screams so as to rouse him: "And what if they wanted to kill me, was it enough?... The devil it was! It was a plot devoid of power both in its military and political impact!" he emphatically rasps out the colorless wording of the Reuter Agency communique, "in Berlin, the plot was stamped out in the very building of the Ministry of War! The soldiers immediately rose in arms in defense of their Fiihrer against the backsliders, to the extent that on leaving their offices apart of them could not even reach the courtyard. The revolted soldiers killed them on the very staircase, do you understand?... On the very staircase! They washed the stairs with their blood!... "

But the effect is reversed. As a soldier, Antonescu understands the reason of blood being shed on the front; as a dictator, he has ordered many an execution himself. But as a man, shedding blood, disgusts him. Therefore he cannot but despise the thirst for blood that excites Hitler's nostrils and makes the hairs of his moustache bristle. He no longer cares for anything. He is not even interested any more in the polite attitude which he has so far imposed upon himself. He poses the question. It was in fact the only important question he had in mind when he came over here to the audience: "Why has the OKW withdrawn so many divisions, particularly the mechanized ones, from the southern front? Does Romania no longer mean anything to the German ally? If my country is required to make such a large contribution in men, weapons, food-stuff and raw materials for supporting the front, why is it left to defend itself and why are the German divisions being withdrawn? Is that what an alliance means?"

Hitler is mild, most surprisingly so. His gaze seems to agree with Antonescu. "You are right," he tells him with a grin of a nondescript nature, "Romania is a great ally of ours, and we, Germany and myself, require much from her just because we trust her!..." He is content as though he had granted an important favor. And he adds relishing the contents of his communication: "Your country is full of fruit and vegetables this season. You ought to give more thought to Germany, who is fighting for you, and send us more supplies. . . " Then, in a tone of mild scolding like that of a parent, he says: " I haven't much felt the taste of Romanian'- fruits and vegetables this year!. . :"

Antonescu refrains himself no longer: - "Let's drop fruits and vegetables! ... Better tell me something definite about the way you are going to assist our front: the front dominated by the Russians who are launching stronger and stronger offensives every day."

....

Further on, the way is described in which Hitler is doped, which leads to strange manifestations of voluntarism and cheerfulness on his part. Antonescu realizes with sadness his domination by a mentally defective person who, unfortunately, has the advantage of the new weapons which were being tested and of information according to which the allied powers had the intention, stipulated, in their agreements, to divide Romania. The Marshal is tormented by the thought of the fate reserved to a small country which is at the mercy of the big powers. He faces Hitler, trying to make him at least pay what is due to Romania for the oil, grains and other goods taken from her.

VIII

The effect of the shot has passed. Hitler is worn out. His gaze is reminiscent of nightmares. "Germany has no debts!" he yells defiantly. "You are our guests to dinner ! . . ."

And he walks out of the rectangular room - a bandaged ghost with limp joints.

Antonescu is disfigured. Completely disfigured. His face has gone blue and death-like with distortion. When he encounters his companions he explains pleadingly: "They want to take everything away from us !". And he shuffles forward dragging his feet with great difficulty along the corridors of that enormous concrete tomb answering absent-mindedly to the salute of the German officers who sense the authoritative and accomplished commander in him.

In their narrow-mindedness they do not understand that all this is futile.

Antonescu had been told once that he enjoyed more military prestige than Hitler himself.

"It stands to reason", the Marshal had answered maliciously, "the Führer is a corporal while I am a soldier!"

But on this day of early August 1944, Ion Antonescu has lost every trace of retort and brightness, every trace of energy. He has a feeling of perplexity, of shame and humiliation which throws him into fits of total prostration.

This feeling abruptly turns into an allergic and vehement hatred when the Baron of Dobmberg, the Reich Head of Protocol, after having knocked at his door, announces him that the Führer feels exhausted by the long interview and hence he will not come to the dinner.

Not wanting to betray his feelings, the Marshal turns his, back to the baron. But after a few minutes, when Mihai Antonescu asks him to come to the reception hall, he screams: "How should I go, if the other one doesn't!?"

The Vice-President of his Council of Ministers tries to soothe him by cracking a joke: "You don't have to be all so scrupulous about it, we shall have Romanian food after all, I mean the food which hasn't been paid for as yet by Dr Clodius."

But the Marshal raps out: "Go and tell them that I will not come !"

And he remains in the concrete cell of his room, staring hatefully at the walls.

IX

The dinner is embarrassing. The four Romanian generals eat very little and do not utter a word. General Steflea, Chief of the Romanian General Staff, from time to time exchanges a few words with Guderian, gazing at his enormous baldness which is somehow compensated for by a thick brushy moustache. If there still is anything like promotion, he and Jodl are the only ones likely to be promoted within the German army. Jodl began his career during the campaign in France, as an artillerist, Guderian in the occupation of Poland, in 1939. Hitler wants them now to cleanse the Wehrmacht of the intellectualist elements. The old general now and again exchanges a word or two with him, as if appraising him, in order to find out the degree of military knowhow concealed under the convexity of his baldness.

Happy and talkative, contrasting with the others, are Keitel and Himmler. Elderly Keitel is jovial, sawing the air like a diplomat in military clothes, and one wouldn't say that he daily kills a few generals or superior officers whose connections with July 20 plotters he discovers. Himmler, with his round steel-rimmed glasses, is surprisingly cheerful. One cannot but wonder what maneuver of the Garman intelligence service makes his face look today like that of a talkative grand-mother eating her favorite cake.

Occupying the seats of honor, in the stead of Hitler and Antonescu, sit Ribbentrop and Mihai Antonescu; they are thoughtful and make no effort to hide it.

The Marshal's palatine, as Mihai Antonescu is dubbed here in the Rastenburg stronghold, has black fakir or self-murderer's - eyes imbued with fright. He has never seen the Marshal so despondent and letting his nerves go in such exasperation. No matter how hard he tries to be amiable to von Ribbentrop, he still does not manage to hide his most tormenting concern that is of hatching all kinds of schemes to save his skin.

The Germans are possessed of a very bad character about him. In the last report sent to Hitler, von Killinger cited among the Führer's opponents: Iuliu Maniu, the leader of the National Peasant Party, an important personality for his connection with the idea of Romania's territorial integrity, the king's mother, Queen Helen, who consistently endeavors to influence her son in favor of a policy of rapprochement towards the Allied Forces, in keeping with the traditional policy of the Romanians, and in the third place, the Vice-President of the Council of Ministers, Mihai Antonescu, a man who was starting more and more evidently

to stand for the interests of the Romanian bourgeoisie anxious to safeguard its positions and who with the elapse of each day was more averse to Romania's alliance with the Axis.

Their suspicion is well-grounded. On the one hand because of the hostile attitude evinced in Romania towards Hitler and his army which is of late becoming more explicit; and on the other hand, on account of the poltroonery and the strings pulled behind the scenes by this academic, by this specialist in international law, amenable and aggressive at the same time, affected and rhetorical in his mode of expression, gliding theatrically with his brillantined long black archangel-like hair through both the policy of the Marshal and that of the Axis.

But, at the same time, it is somewhat exaggerated to categorize him as an opponent of the Marshal, together with the queen and with Iuliu Maniu. It is true that he sinuates, that he perfumes himself beautifully and has a pedantic command over the language, and endeavors to save his neck in case of the Marshal's downfall. He favors people who might have him in view later and he is even tempted to betray the Marshal unscrupulously so as to take over his place. But he is supported in all this by the Romanian public opinion where the incongruity of this alliance is openly discussed as being neither in keeping with the tradition nor with Romanian aspirations, but merely the outcome of a historical moment when the nation had been threatened too seriously by other countries.

But to go so far as to categorize this tragi-comical character with his policy and versatility - thoroughly studied over the years, and minutely described by moralists as belonging to a classical psychological category - as being an opponent, the drunken stupidity of one like von Killinger was necessary.

A successful lawyer with curly hair and beige silk shirts, an academic eager to make a brilliant career, who ever since he has been Vice-President of the Council of Ministers has had his collections of prolix words printed in luxurious editions intended to impress the diplomats who visit him, just like provincial lawyers who receive their rural clients in sumptuous libraries full of unread books in order to extort larger fees from them, Mihai Antonescu had had the chance to be chosen by the Marshal as ideologist to a military government which was not very keen on having a well-outlined political conception. He knows that. He knows he is looked down upon by the true intellectuals, but he guts ahead of the latter by playing up to certain high and mighty persons. And on no account can he be Antonescu's opponent. He is at most an experienced politician, ready to betray in order to secure a future position for himself, ready to jump out of trouble at the very last moment lest he should sink with the ship.

But von Killinger had personal reasons for accusing him: An adventurer and an iron hand by nature, during World War I, he had been commander of a submarine and Hitler's personal friend, he had been involved in the plot on the life of King Alexander of Yugoslavia and supervisor of German interests in the Balkan-Danubian area, having supervised this part of Europe, first from Bratislava and later from Bucharest. The German Ambassador was a typically faithful member of the Nazi Party: unsociable, soldierly, rendering his complexes into acts of terror and quenching his thirst for horror by drinking. Sulky and contemptuous, an addict to alcohol and narcissist to the extent of hanging his own portrait above his desk, he was a man who was suffering terribly in Romania on account of his indefinite and delicate status. Just like the German Ambassadors in other countries, he considered it his right to play the Teutonic absolute master. Only that he was compelled to consume his authoritative pretensions in secret, because Ion Antonescu with his stern prestige of an experienced military commander had the upper hand. He dominated him and roused an inferiority complex in hint and made him tremble respectfully in the cadence of the most military Prussian discipline. "You are the only German Ambassador in these countries who puts out his cigar and rectifies his carriage when entering the office of the local head of state," Göring had once mocked at him, wishing to prove that he was in possession of complete information. Out of spite, von Killinger avoided talking to the Marshal in as much as it was possible. He would appease his inferiority complex by filling his car with brandy, and by spending his time at bear-hunting parties. And since protocol contacts, were required of him and he wished to avoid the feeling that the austere man of arms, the Romanian head of state, dominated his hulking bulk of a body bent towards earthly pleasures, he had started to call on Mihai Antonescu ever more frequently.

But only after a few months he became envious of him: his military Prussian mind could not make anything out of the sophisticated sentences uttered by this Levanto-Latin prestidigitator who was the Vice-President of the Romanian Council of Ministers. Von Killinger had come to understand with great difficulty not only that he could not make out what his interlocutor was saying, but that sometimes his leg was being pulled by the latter's empty phraseology. And when this opinion got stuck in his rigid Teutonic mind, stressing the fact that he had been made a fool of, nothing could held back his hatred. He lay in wait for hint. He lay in wait for him for a long time, while drinking quantities of brandy, as he used to do when lying in ambush for hunting bears. And when he caught him dealing with Bova Scoppa, the Italian diplomatic representative, who later declared himself to be on general Badoglio's side, he spared him no longer; he took revenge for Mihai Antonescu's verbal sophistication, and also for the sense of inferiority the Marshal stirred in him; he discredited him everywhere by calling him a traitor and, the previous year, he had even gone so far as to determine Hitler to ask the Marshal to take steps against him.

The assertion that Mihai Antonescu was an opponent of Marshal Ion Antonescu had proved to be somewhat hazardous and revealed what a bad politician and what an incompetent diplomat von Killinger was both to those who knew it already and to those who held him in esteem. And his absence from the present interview was yet another confirmation of this widespread opinion about him. General Hansen, head of the German Mission in Bucharest is accompanying the Marshal in his place. Like a little obedient mouse, he is sitting at the far end of the table, waiting for the dinner to be over so as to go and call upon one of his mistresses who was especially invited to wait for him in a little hotel near Rastenburg.

But the other Germans are closely watching the dark-haired man who is sitting in silence on the right hand side of von Ribbentrop. They know that in a way Mihai Antonescu is the Marshal's invention and therefore they wonder how he can also be his opponent. They are not relatives, although considering the name one would be tempted to think so. In his capacity of a lawyer he assisted him both in a queer law-suit of bigamy, about which nobody knew anything definite; and in the law-suit which ended for the Marshal with his being placed under house arrest. Later he stayed on as a sort of private secretary of the Marshal, Ion Antonescu was a man who had no associates and preferred to employ people who merely executed his orders. After the iron guards uprising of 1941 when Horia Sima, who- had, been the Vice-President of the Council of Ministers, fled the country aided by the Germans, and Mihai Sturza, former iron-guards Minister of Foreign Affairs followed suit, the Marshal to be had no better alternative than to choose Mihai Antonescu, known by the nickname of Ica, as his assistant. After the stamping out of the iron-guard upheaval, when Antonescu formed a new government based on repressive bodies and on an exceptional legislation, he appointed Mihai Antonescu as Vice-President of the Council of Ministers, and for the periods of his absence while inspecting the front, ‚ad-interim Prime Minister.

At mid-half of the 20th century la Antonescu, attempting to improvise an ideology empty of any content, barring the interests of the handful of people growing rich by the war, concealed the lack of ideas by means of a sophisticated terminology imitating the language of bygone centuries. His sentences resembled the present-day ceremonies at royal courts, ceremonies which cultivated monarchs strive to turn into modern parties by affecting a sporting behavior.

But they, Ion Antonescu and his paladin, were the representatives, at least instinctively so, as they had not had the time to establish their ideational platform, of the ossifying tendencies of the bourgeoisie which was attempting to conceal its corrupt adventurous past by an outward show of nobleness. The military haughtiness and the clannish ceremonial of a caste like nature which were imposed by the Marshal's dictatorship were very much to the taste of the upstart bourgeoisie which wished to impose itself both as a traditional and a leading upper class. These aspects conferred to the Romanian society a conservative existence with a touch of mysticism to it, behind which one could count on the stability of big capital business and the stability of the people's religious and patriotic feeling.

In this respect it was quite clear for them as to whose interests they should devote themselves: "Day in and day out I fight for the Romanian bourgeoisie. Day in and day out it is to it that I delicate all my faith", Mihai Antonescu wrote in Statements of General Policy. While Ion Antonescu, in the proclamation of the 6 November plebiscite, in 1941, declared to the entire nation: "The new -Romanian State should devote all its efforts to the molding and the strengthening of our bourgeoisie."

This was the puny political platform they had in common, common even in the conservatory tenor in which they each spoke about the people and the active bourgeoisie in a conservative manner when thinkers the world over were much more cautious in their estimates, irrespective whether they were exaggerating it in a so cold revolutionary spirit or whether they were bantering it on account of what its existence demolished in human nobleness.

Antigauchiste, justified by the Bolshevik danger near our boundaries, but, in the same time, opposite to the iron-guard fascism, Ica Antonescu had never had the courage to attempt the overthrow of this puny platform. He had only endeavored to ensure the possibility for himself of jumping over on to another one in case of need. In his churlish folly, Hitler's personal friend, Baron von Killinger, who was most obviously no diplomat and could in no way play the role of the protector of Romania in the presence of Ion Antonescu by exposing his qualities of a satrap, underrated Mihai Antonescu by ranking his policies as adversities.

Mihai Antonescu protected the envoys of the National-Peasant and National-Liberal political parties sent abroad and saw it that Maniu and Bratianu were informed as to the intelligence received through diplomatic channels. And ever since Prince Barbu Stirbey, former lover of Queen Mary, former President of the Council of Ministers and the personal enemy of Charles II, had left for Constantinople in possession of a diplomatic passport given to him with the personal assent of the Marshal in order to sound the English-American circles and to discuss with them the eventual possibilities of Romania's egress from the war, he, Ica, had put at their disposal the secret code service to enable certain communications they needed. For this purpose he appointed Grigore Niculescu-Buzesti, the son-in-law of Prince Stirbey, as director of the code in the Foreign Affairs Ministry. The Germans watched over his house with colonnades built of fret worked stone in Bucharest, as well as over his rather modest bourgeois villa at Butimanu where he was stowing away reserves of English and American currency taken as bribes from the Jews he had delivered from the concentration camps. And as Romania was the only country in which, a big part of the Jews eluded going to camps, Mihai Antonescu's reserves at the villa on the shore of the modest lowland lake were slowly piling up. In July he had sold his house in Batistei street, changing the received sum into Swiss money. For this reason the head of the press department in the German Ministry of Foreign Affairs, Paul Schmidt, had declared that two people in Bucharest would not let him sleep in peace: Ica

Antonescu and Pamfil Seicaru, a great newspaperman who used to declare himself to be pro-German, but who was also amassing English and American currency.

Only once had Mihai Antonescu confronted von Killinger openly, that was in the case of Bova Scopa, the diplomat who has made arrangements for his visit to Italy and for his dealing with the Holy See. Bova Scopa was the diplomatic representative of Italy, an intimate friend of count Ciano who, in September 1943, had declared himself in favor of the pro-Allied government formed by General Badoglio. The German Embassy requested that Bova Scopa be instantly confined to a camp. Mihai Antonescu refused and allowed him to continue inhabiting the white building with its classical platform, property of the Italian Embassy. Furthermore, he didn't interfere in any way when the new plenipotentiary appointed by Mussolini could not enter the Embassy over Bova Scopa's head. The events took a most unfortunate turn because chance had it that the buffoonery should take, place in a most unique setting: the Italian Embassy in Bucharest occupied a house built back to back with the building of the German Embassy. Only a thick wall surrounding the gardens separated them. In order to enter his own Embassy, Mussolini's new envoy was forced to climb over the wall in the backyard of the German Embassy, and to fight hand-to-hand with Bova Scopa. They fought like two carousers breaking the Venetian mirrors and the Murano glass, because count Ciano's man, knowing himself to be protected, stood his ground. Mihai Antonescu interfered only to require that Bova Scopa be granted the permission to leave for Italy unhindered.

Completely non-Latin and malignantly reacting upon this kind of nice superficiality, mind-limited because his lack of imagination, but persevering and vain, like an awkward fencing-fighter using a cannon against his adversary, Killinger found revenge in the papers of a full file.

At the Munich meeting of 1943, Ion Antonescu was shown a complete file regarding all the dubious dealings Mihai Antonescu was trying to carry through in his various connections with the Allies. The Marshal was forced to promise Hitler that he would release him from his functions, and therefore he returned to Romania in a very bad state of mind for, although some of Ica's maneuvers had been made with his approval, the greater part of the information received had astounded him. Among other things he found out about a proposal made by Ica to Carlton Hayes, the U.S. ambassador in Madrid, in which he declared himself ready to sign, on behalf of the Romanian government, a declaration of capitulation. And, in addition, this capitulation was to be made to the Turkish government!...

In response to the harsh reproaches of the Marshal - and understanding, in his capacity of a lawyer, that the disclosure of his actions could lead even to a death sentence - Mihai Antonescu fell to his knees shedding tears profusely and assuring him that he had tried all those schemes only to safeguard him, the Marshal, their common policy, and their common interests. And on realizing after long pleadings that they would never succeed in dissuading the Marshal, he changed his lawyer's verbiage into the language of a hairdresser unhappy in love and asked the Marshal's permission to commit suicide. Believing him to be sincere, the Marshal was impressed since Ica had had several cases of suicide in his family. Accordingly, he took no other steps against him. He treated him contemptuously, leaving him to regulate his dealings with afterlife by his own means and ways.

Ica lay ill for about a month, brooding over the promised suicide. When he reappeared he looked thin and tormented and he declared that it was only his conscience of a loyal follower of the Marshal that had prevented him from laying violent hands on himself, for that would have meant deserting the Marshal in this most trying moment for the war and for the nation. Ion Antonescu was not happy about this decision but, being a Christian, he could not bring himself to sage Mihai Antonescu to commit suicide.

The Marshal lacked the disposition or the strength to punish him anymore, while at Hitler's headquarters matters were left to rest as their entire attention was focused upon the grave situation on the front during the 1943 winter.

Reports about him continued to arrive reading: that he was frequently visited by Suphy Tanrioer, the ambassador of Turkey to Bucharest; that together with Mrs. Antonescu, the Marshal's wife who, in spite of the queen mother, would entitle herself the first lady of the country, she was doing business through the instrumentality of the so-called Patronage Agency, completely discrediting the Marshal's good name - he whose great merit was the honesty of a poor saint which he obstinately preserved unblemished; that he issued written notes for the setting free of each Jew, thus preparing documents which would speak in his favor in a time when the Nazis might be overthrown; that, among the various academies he had founded for the purpose of patronizing them and endowing himself with the aura of a mecena, he had also set up the academy of the diplomats, a site where he had tried to speak well of Titulescu's policy; that for the same reason he had promoted to the Ministry of Foreign Affairs Titulescu's former principal secretary, Grigore Niculescu-Buzesti, known to be pro-British and at the same time Barbu Stirbey's son-in-law; that through the agency of Turkey he worked towards putting himself under the protection of the Allied forces Command in Cairo, sounding both Lord Moyne, the English representative, and McVeigh, the American representative, etc., etc., etc.

Fact is that, as here, near Balkans, where nothing is taken so seriously, the Marshal and some of his generals being the self-persons taken seriously in this government, Ica was harmless. His Mephistophelian smile and his absent-minded and mysterious manners were highlighted by his deftly employing an ambiguous language, interspersed with quotations having nothing to do with the subject of conversation, and intended merely to set off his knowledge. Thus his qualities as a diplomat had to be recognized because there would be no knowing whether he was using these quotations to prevent the debates from arriving at concrete solutions or whether, on the contrary, he was robbing the conversation of purpose, conducting it in a way that would enable him to employ his quotations. This dilemma, in fact, put to the test von Killinger's slow mind, making him rave with fury that Ica was poking fun at him by means of his slippery language.

"However, I need Ica", the Marshal once declared, seeking an apology, "he has oratorical qualities and I cannot waste my time with inaugurations, festivities and burials. He holds the speeches on my behalf."

Thus, due to the situation on the front, as well as to his lack of will-power which Antonescu felt growing within him, although he strove to conceal it from others, "the Ica case" was hushed up. And as the Marshal used to spend three days a week on the front, he was unable to find anyone more appropriate for the position of temporary Prime Minister.

From this to the position of permanent Prime Minister these was but one step. An essential on, but still only one step. Mihai Antonescu sought to assure himself of the fact that the establishment of a long-wished-for peace would stress the Marshal's inadequacy as head of state. That is why he was so impatient and why he increased his innovating schemes tenfold. He once even dared, in March 1944, to tell the Marshal: "The whole country wants peace!..." which was only the expression of his impatience to see himself at the head of the government.

Ion Antonescu retaliated violently: "You are not the country; I am the country !" - And here, in the bunker of Rastenburg, sitting by the champagne glasses filled with Deutcher Sekt - which nobody touches any longer except for Himmler whose face is all flushed like that of a military assistant doctor's, and for Keitel who is holding his glass between his elegant fingers - the dinner offers no opportunity for Mihai Antonescu to put into operation any of his maneuvers. Quite on the contrary, considering the Marshal's blind and impotent fury and the fact that, instead of coming to table, Hitler, all wrapped up in his bandages, is shivering somewhere in the bunker, he has many more chances of being sent directly into an extermination camp and being turned into soap.

So he simply holds a formal diplomatic conversation with von Ribbentrop, that is a conversation without subjects or predicates and, at the end of the dinner, he rises quickly as if from an electric chair, happy to have escaped execution.

But as soon as he shakes off the obsession, the very moment he returns among his own kith and kin to the Marshal's rooms, he recovers his impudence and says: "I yelled at von Ribbentrop: It can't go on like this, your Excellency, it can't go on like this any longer !..."

Highly dignified, with his bushy white moustache, General Steflea, who has long warned the Marshal that Ica must be somebody's spy, cannot refrain anymore. And when they withdraw leaving their leader to sleep, he stops him on the corridor and fells him point blank: "How dare you, sir, lie like a trooper?! We were together when you talked to von Ribbentrop and I didn't hear you say anything like that!"

Ica is not impressed nor taken aback in the least. His instincts, those of a true descendant of Uriah Heep, react promptly. In a solemn tone he puts the old distinguished gentleman into his place: "General, sir, I for one, cherish nobody more than the Marshal. I prefer even to strain the truth, only to see him a little calmer, more at ease!... What I said was uttered with the definite purpose of helping him to fall asleep more easily."

And he smiles an oily charming smile bidding them all good night.

....

XI

It is a clear morning and the middle of Europe - that Mitteleuropa - over which the plane is now flying is perfectly visible with all its open wounds inflicted by the long war. The plains are burnt to ashes, the rivers broadened in the places where the now blown-up bridges used to be, the settlements demolished. It is only the verdure of the forests, which from place to place stirs the emotion of natural existence in one's heart.

The plane keeps flying indefinitely over a continental Europe marked by the arrow-like spires of catholic churches or by the white turrets of baroque churches which shepherd the villages clustering round them. Owing to the trenches and the fortifications and the bomb craters which put a macabre stamp on the entire landscape consisting of war-weary meadows and low wooded hills, one cannot tell exactly where one is. And yet a feeling of uneasiness is creeping over each of the passengers. Everything seems most unfamiliar to them, the course the plane is flying seems most bizarre while its direction rouses anxiety all round. The Marshal and his entourage cast more and more frequent glances at their watches and start to fidget in their seats, despite the fact that the pilots who have come from the front assure them that the direction of the plane is the required one and that they are following the safest itinerary, the best defended one.

Until all of a sudden, below them the sky is all afire. A little time must first elapse before they get used to it and come to understand that they are flying very low over a burning city.

The: aides de camp go up to the German pilots and admonish them, but they answer that they have acted according to their orders. The plane is flying over Warsaw. They will fly over the city twice, after which the plane will make headway for Bucharest. After having been told about their whereabouts, Antonescu understands. He nods showing that he has understood, refraining himself as much as possible, but he cannot control his emotions and he blurts out: "It was Hitler who gave this order!... They, have made this detour to show us what they have brought Warsaw to. Look: it's all flames and ruins!... He forced us to make this detour with the definite purpose of warning us that the same may happen to Bucharest if ... "

He stops short, swallowing a gulp in his throat. He does not define more accurately the nature of the "if".

He lapses into an absurd silence, a corollary of the blurred irresponsibility which has seized him.

Below them Warsaw is burning with huge, criminal flames. The roaring of guns and shell bursts are heard, because Hitler has not contented himself with setting fire to it. He has located on each street either a gun or a flame-thrower, demolishing and burning it down in a diabolically organized manner, with a perfect German technique.

Hitler's idea has attained its purpose. Antonescu is completely shaken. The sharp features of his profile have grown soft and weak; he feels the whole world weighing upon his shoulders. He comes to his senses only when they are above Bucharest, but surveying it from that height he sees it all ablaze. And this image harasses him to such an extent that the feels unable to remain in the capital. He leaves immediately for Olanesti to treat his badly shaken nervous system.

Iuliu Maniu declared: "I agree to finish this war; I agree the idea that the alliance with Hitler was a conjectural one; but I want guarantees; I need guarantees... I need the guarantees of the Allied Forces. Bring me the guarantees of Mr. Stalin, Mr. Roosevelt and Mr. Churchill..

II. THE TWENTY-SECOND OF AUGUST AND ITS ANTECEDENTS

Bucharest, Romania's capital city, is described, with its life during the war. Aspects of the population's everyday life, the hostile attitude towards Hitler's troops, the European traditions of the cultural and spiritual life, the democratic nature of political life which stands up to the military dictatorship, aspects of the official, government activities and of the clandestine activities which led to the emergence of the National Block.

In a secret house, at 113 Mosilor Road, the finishing touches are put to a plan for a political overthrow planned for the weekend, Saturday, August 26, at 12 hours, the time of the break for lunch in all units, according to the strict regulations of the German army.

A historical outline of the anti-dictatorial movement is made, followed by a presentation of the ways and means which led to the political platform of the Democratic National Block and of the biographies of some leaders and militants: The chiefs of the outlaw historical parties abolished by the dictatorship of the former king Carol the second; the camarilla of the young king Michael and his supposed flirt with the Nazi iron-guard; the traditional moderate communists face to the dangerous lack of ideology of the Moscow's agents commando and them fight for priority in this little party becoming significant only thanks to the offensive of the Red army; the attitude of some generals and the dissatisfaction in the Romanian army, etc. And, not at last, the dream of the

Romanian population " to see coming here the Americans", with the signification to be no more at the mercy of the neighbor aggressive powers.

A review is made of the increasingly firm actions of the last three years through which the democratic movement achieved the coalition of the internal forces and, at the indication of the Allies Forces, founded a connection with some communists, expecting from them part to join the interests of Moscow which approve of negotiations only with the Marshal Antonescu.

The details are established for the political act which is going to be accomplished by the military units which will participate to the King's proclamation broadcasted on the radio. Written by the communist traditional militant Lucretiu Patrascanu, at his suggestion, the proclamation was recorded before, to have the record in case he, the king, disappears or is kidnaped. So, the army will hear the voice of them symbolic commander and the conspirators will be sure that the soldiers will action.

Nicknamed "the Queer Bird", this Patrascanu is more a national free thinker orientate to the left, not involved in the actions of other so-called communists - in fact, Kremlin's agents. Coming from a cultured family of publicists, barrister defending the political defendants in the inter-war period trials, nine years later, he will be killed by his "comrades".

Portraits of characters from both camps. Hitler's staff, the two Antonescu, Killinger, Hansen, Gerstemberg, some political leaders with a half-underground activity, chiefs of secret services and military or civil policemen, German SS, Russian provokers, incendiaries or vanguard secret agents, Italian deserters and British spies, officers of the Royal House an Public Protocol, conservative academic people and patriots volunteers on the front, public persons, artists, intellectuals, journalists, coffee houses and newspapers offices of Bucharest, the pubs and the restaurants of the former "Little Paris", all is described as the place becoming the revolving base plate of the second world war.

Four other characters must be mentioned:

The Antonescu's relations with the Palace are ensured by General Constantin Sanatescu, A cavalry officer and a Military-school colleague of Ion Antonescu's, he had been entrusted with this important function in the Royal House by the Marshal himself. He had been assigned to this task a year before, early in 1943, when the serious disagreements between the Palace and the dictator had occurred. And the dictator had delegated his old schoolmate to keep watch over the mother queen's vain gloriousness and the king's youth menaced by some adventurers of his camarilla and the former flirt with the iron-guard, which chief, Horia Sima, is kept by Hitler in Germany as alternative at the form of government if Antonescu become uncertain and must be changed. A distinguished officer, General Sanatescu had been accepted by the royal family as Chief of the Military Royal House. And now, a year later, being lucid by nature, he comes to understand both the inexorable necessity for the country to be rid of Antonescu and the need for himself to co-operate with the conspiracy against the connection Antonescu – Hitler and the obstinate old-fashion military honesty of the Marshal.

The most important civilian character is Iuliu Maniu, a very big and important Transylvanian nationalist, with indisputable merits in the fulfillment of the Great Romania in 1918, former Prime Minister in the '33 crisis' period, absolutely recognized as leader of the National-Peasant movement or party, even after its dictatorial abolition and, in the same time, a person having old strong relations with London. Growing old, his prestige increased and, to a great extent, increased his political abilities, very advisable in such discretional-dictatorial or, also, conspirative-discreet situations. He organized meetings in the houses of his adherents and participate at others; but temporizing and taking his liberty to make his own analysis and calculations, such that he discouraged the young royal camarilla feeling enthusiasm for the landing of the Marshall and the turn of the weapons, with his stereotype formula: "I am waiting for suggestions of London; I want London's guarantee". And, as London recommended us to keep in contact with Moscow, the evolution of the events was temporized. At Cairo, the English representative, Lord Moyne and USA representative, McVeigh recommended to the special emissary, Prince Stirbey, to keep the contact with Novikov, the Soviet representative. From London, the same message through the agency of a transmitter used by three English officers parachuted in Romania and hided by Romanian army to be not arrested by the Gestapo. And, on secret ways, arrives details on the Churchill-

Stalin agreement of 1943, concerning the after war's distribution of the influence zones on the map of Central and South-East Europe: Greece for England, Romania for the Soviets. Experimented in connections with London before and in the time of the firs World War, when the Big Powers had an interest for the strategic Down Danube and for the Romanian petroleum, face to the new geopolitical situation, Iuliu Maniu hides himself behind a sinuous style of political behavior. Putting things off, is with him an illness, it seems. But, owing to the political ability with which he safeguards his private interests as well as those of his party, it is a disease which suits both his purposes and those of his followers. A shortcoming which he has turned into an advantage, a physic incapacity rendered into a perfidious political weapon. Always protracting and canvassing, Iuliu Maniu had never succeeded in marrying, forever deferring and seeking, he had not managed over a quarter of a century, since he had come to Bucharest, to settle down in a dwelling-place, invariably lodging – the poor drifting soul – in the home of various supporters or relatives. Anecdote has it that one day he made up his mind to have a house built in Bucharest, so he appointed an architect to draft the building plans. When they were ready, he required whether the lavatory would be built on the ground floor or on the first floor, wherever he decided. Maniu kept putting him off for years, telling him that he had not yet thought it over sufficiently to take the decision as regards where the lavatory should be located… Debating and protracting, Maniu represents a great incertitude for the conspiratorial activity which should operate like clock-work, should be carried out in conditions of secrecy and certitude, should each and every day achieve the scheduled aims and should attain the degree of preparedness, that should render possible at the slightest notice the triggering off of the overthrow. With his and others political platform support and the cooperation of the military forces, it may be a movement saving us by both occupations: Hitler's or Stalin's. Without it, it will be only an uncertain Palace-plot or coup d'état. And, anyway, the old politician doesn't want to take the risk to involve his person.

    The third and the forth characters are Dinu Bratianu, chief of the National-Liberal party, descendant of the famous liberal family Bratianu and Constantin Titel Petrescu chief of the Social-

Democrats. They were involved in the events of August 1944 and in the governments installed after and had the same cruel destiny as Maniu, to be plunged into the Bolshevik's hard-jails.

It is the conflict situation and its characters on the revolving base plate of the second world war which became Bucharest in that August month.

At the end of the hot day of 22th, take place the arrival of Clodius, the German representative for south-east Europe, a first meeting between him and Mihai Antonescu to explore one-other, completed with shorts interviews with the Marshall in the middle of other its preoccupations as Supreme Commander and the fixing of a special meeting between Clodius and Marshal Antonescu, to review the entire situation, scheduled for the afternoon of the following day: August 23 1944.

XXVII

More than a year, after Stalingrad, Maniu declared: "I agree to finish this war; I agree the idea that the alliance with Hitler was a conjectural one; but I want guarantees; I need guarantees... I need the guarantees of the Allied Forces. Bring me the guarantees of Mr. Stalin, Mr. Roosevelt and Mr. Churchill..."

To his amazement, in the end, he received the confirmation of the Allies. And, moreover, he received it by the agency of the very men he himself had accredited! ... In Cairo, Prince Stirbey and Constantin Visoianu contacted both the representatives of the three Powers: Lord Moyne - The United Kingdom. McVeigh - The United States and Novikov - The Soviet Union, and General Wilson, the Commander in Chief of the Allied Forces in the Mediterranean area. On 12 April, Novikov communicated both to the Antonescu government and to Mr. Iuliu Maniu the following conditions for an armistice:

1. The breaking off of relations with Germany and the participation of the Romanian Army in the joint struggle alongside the Allies and the Red Army against the Germans, with a view to establishing Romania's independence and sovereignty.

2. The re-establishment of the Soviet-Romanian frontier existing at the end of June 1940.

3. The payment of damages due to the prejudices brought about by the Romanians in their occupying Soviet territory.

4. The handing over of all Soviet and Allied Forces prisoners as well as all Soviet subjects detained in Romania.

5. The warranting of the free passage of Soviet and Allied forces troops on Romania's territory in case the military situation should so require. To this purpose the Romanian Government would as far as possible place at their disposal all the necessary means of communication by land, water and air.

b. The Soviet Government agrees to the cancellation of the stipulation incorporated in the Vienna Diktat concerning Transylvania and assures Romania of its assistance with a view to liberating Transylvania.

Reasoning that these harsh conditions for the country were partly due to himself, at the following meeting Iuliu Maniu was sincere: He did not even attempt to sketch a thought about the nation and its destiny, telling point-blank: "My dear fellows, why should we be fools and assume the risks? Antonescu got the country into the war, so let Antonescu get it out of it!"... Upon which, Lucretiu Patrascanu retorted: "Mr Maniu, I knew you to be a great patriot, but really this is overdoing it!... " Maniu did not answer him; he became ceremonious on hearing the attribute he was so fond of hearing and uttered: "Well, you must know, my dear fellow, that my patriotism is known far and wide, and your own father wrote about it in the newspapers of Wallachia and Moldavia at a time when I was taking great pains to display it in the presence of foreigners, in Budapest".

Becoming grave and paying attention to the discussion, with the mien of the truly lucid and perspicuous politician that ho was, Maniu renounced his subtle mask of slight detachment, slight state of tiredness and old age incapable of concentration, arguing energetically: "I backed him because it was the only solution for the country and it was the only policy, the only system of alliance by virtue of which we could hope for re-uniting the frontiers...Believe me, I am an experienced politician, and I have once before brought Transylvania back to its mother land. I had no need for demonstrations, and bringing order into chaos was at that time more necessary for a country subjected to all kinds of confusions. Much more necessary, even though it was being brought about by means of a sword, towards which was were later to express our reserves."

Patrascanu smiled his malicious smile, trying to make Marxist education to the young men of the royal camarilla aware of the Allies order to co-operate with the communists: "And you encouraged, as Marx says about Cavaignac, Not a dictatorship of the sword over the bourgeois society, but a bourgeois dictatorship by the sword." These words made the old Maniu admit frankly: "Yes, indeed, I did bring him to that in the end - let us turn him into the instrument of a necessity of the present moment and then let us confine ourselves to..."

His speech was no longer high-flown, he no longer repeated either his verbal mannerisms or his favorite phrases, and he did not give that presumptuous priority to the Latin-Transylvanian terminology as was his custom. He had dropped all the semblances of the arsenal which his lengthy political experience had amassed and behaved like an extremely perspicuous man, well aware of what he was about and of what he deliberated, guided by a most accurate reasoning as concerns the interests of the policy he had devoted himself to and by means of which both he and his country had equally benefited. Sensing his most welcome sincerity, Patrascanu urged him, as had been his purpose from the first: "Well, confine yourself! What else am I asking you to do?. . ."

Feeling that he is to corner because of the threat of the Red Pover in the East-side, Maniu answered not shrinking from giving himself as an example: "Well, I did confine myself; the instant Antonescu crossed the Dniester, I drew his attention for the need to stop; we had no right to venture further; the rest of it is an adventure which I do not countenance. So, let him sign the armistice, not I. I told him to stop, my dear fellows!... What, do you not believe in my circumspections?!..."

....

A picture is given of the protracted talks among the parties, the personalities and the military people making up the Democratic National Block for establishing the membership of a new government to come into office after the planned action as well as of the diplomatic moves of the representatives of the National Block and - also, in parallels, at the same time of the Marshal Antonescu's government - in Stockholm and Cairo, for talks with the allied powers. With a view to the proposed overthrow and turn of the weapons against the former German ally, these diplomatic moves represents many kinds of interests: From the Antonescu's opposition to Hitler's selfish strategy, to the patriotic aspiration to save to the greatest extent the country's sovereignty, but passing by the specific interest of the political parties, of the king and his mother, of the Royal Court, of the Government or of the Army in them entities or in everyone component person selfish, etc. Only the population, in all its majority traditional menaced by the imperial German or Russian danger, waits and hope "To arrive the Americans", don't being able to understand the Roosevelt's sensibility and naïve attraction for Stalin, for the Soviets and for the Slav instinct of domination in this part of the world.

The King leaves his castle in Sinaia and arrives in Bucharest to effectively participate in the last secret preparations.

The situation on the front and the measures taken by the German Command to ensure an increased resistance in the context of the uncertain situation in Romania are reported by the German secret services.

The plans of resistance and front retirement worked out by Marshal Antonescu rely upon the fortified line in the middle of the country (Focsani-Namoloasa-Galati). Such a measure could lead to the country's division into two parts, saving the South-one to be able to wait for the Anglo-American forces of the Mediterranean area, but leaving the North-one in the hands of Stalin. It would have suited the foreign political and military forces, especially the shortest direction of the Red Army to Berlin and the arrival to Danube of the Allied Forces from Greece, but would have led to a national disaster breaking the Romania's territory and proroguing a fracture for the Romanian people (as, in part it has happen with Basarabia).

For this reason, calculating that he will accept to remain ruler over a part of the country, the Soviets prefer to negotiate with Antonescu. Such is underlined the lucidity of the underground patriot fighters who, realizing that was exactly what Antonescu's plans and the advance of the Soviet troops pursued, take the decision to act only in the national interest of the country's unity.

XXXVIII

Below, on the airport, Mihai Antonescu, the Marshal's paladin, his Deputy Premier in the leadership of the Council of Ministers, Premier ad-interim whenever the Marshal is away on the front, therefore also now, for yet another minute or so, until the plane lands, has much the same thoughts flitting, through his mind.

Very much the same but reverse, for Ica is brooding over how he could possibly seam more affectionate and respectful at the same time, how he could acquire a sincerely concerned and attentive mien to everything the Marshal might tell him, a mien which should reveal his great happiness at seeing his upholder and mentor and also his great eagerness to receive his advice.

In order to conceal the concerns and especially the fears which stir him to the bottom of his heart, he turns his attention to his appearance, he carefully smooth his sleekly combed hair, he presses down his thick hypnotizer-like eyebrows and looks narcissistically at the door crystals in which his swarthy complexion and perfectly shaven cheeks set off by a faultless silk collar are reflected.

All this because his instinct of self-preservation prompts him to conceal, even from his own self, the tormenting thought of betraying the Marshal. And he must betray him as soon as possible. Before it is too late. Before the whole country, which is already in an advanced state of unrest, rises in revolt.

"As soon as possible! Or otherwise . . ."

No, no, he has no scruples. "It's a long time since I gave up having any scruples," he thinks to himself. He had been, there was no denying it, faithful as long as he had felt Antonescu's position unshaken. But to carry on any longer ... Mihai Antonescu's spiritual make-up was such that in his relations with other people he felt no urge to be sincere to anybody. Temperamentally versatile, he was, like all intelligent, intellectual social climbers, well-armed with a thick glaze of borrowed words and ide-as. So thick a glaze that it was not only difficult to reach its mettle but also to tell whether it contained anything at all.

Now, indeed, he has every reason to think more about his own predicament than about the Marshal's. The situation is of such a nature that if there are arguments in favor of the military commander's pursuing a status-quo policy, for himself, as a politician, there would be no excuse for overlooking the slightest opportunity to break away from Hitler and the dictatorship.

As a matter of fact, he has known it ever since 1943; since he acted in the manner of a bold, far-sighted diplomat, by trying to induce Mussolini to break away from Germany together with him; on which occasion Hitler's men labeled him as a British-American spy and, alongside Pamfil Seicaru, he has been enlisted as the first among the most dangerous and the most liable to commit treason, from among those who ranked high in the favor of the dictatorship.

Deep in thought, Mihai Antonescu paces leisurely to and from in front of the small group of generals who have accompanied him to the airport, dressed in his black outfit which makes him look like a flashy entertainer in an exclusive night club, he endeavors through the grave silent mood he has assumed to resemble as closely as possible a stoic philosopher, the more so, as his inner concerns, are of a very utilitarian nature.

In fact, the Marshal himself - he tries to justify his thoughts - is looking for an opportunity to shake off Hitler's chains. The Marshal too is negotiating with the Russians and is seeking to gain General Wilson's goodwill... The only thing is that he is trying to delay the armistice as long as possible, reasoning that the right moment must be chosen very carefully. As for himself, for Mihai Antonescu, any moment is the right one. Positively so. If only an opportunity would turn up or if only the feelers he has put out would receive an answer... A little answer!... Oh, how he wished he had succeeded then in prevailing upon Mussolini!... He would suave played the trump card of his life!

He frowns but he represses any impulsive gesture lest he should cause his companions to smile. As a matter of fact, in as far as the Marshal is concerned, Ion Antonescu, Ionel, as he had come to call him in the years of their close intimacy at the beginnings of the dictatorship, he had done his duty by him long ago, ever since that March when he had quite emphatically told him that the country wanted peace... "You are not the country! I am the country!" the Marshal had replied quite harshly, allowing his pent-up hatred to break out, a hatred brought about by, his not having replaced Mihai when circumstances demanded it.

As a consequence of his selfish sensitivity, Mihai Antonescu had felt hart: after all why shouldn't he "be the country" too, and why should the other man be?!... This was only a short-lived reaction because Iei Antonescu is more realistic than the Marshal, for the latter has grown convinced of the fact that he really "is the country", and bears this attribute with an unvanquished serenity.

In fact, his resentment was the outcome of much deeper feelings than the mere ambition of sharing with the Marshal something that could not possibly belong to either of them. It was his definite conviction, his deep-rooted belief that if this obstinate officer, harsh and styled, but one-sided in point of thinking, had come to consider himself to be the father, the savior of the country, or even the country itself, then all this was-due only to him, to Mihai Antonescu, due to his competent policy, due to his skill in making a wide-ranging propaganda for him in such a short period of time.

The Marshal was conceited to the extent of having come to draw his attention to certain titles or qualities of his, which might all be taken in earnest only by the wide public, by the soldiers and by the average citizens, but not by his close friends, and especially not by him, he who had invented them and who had had the skill to impose them upon the public opinion.

He was right in feeling offended because Ion Antonescu, the saint, the hero, the national genius, as he is described in the official documents, was his invention, and only a great lawyer like himself, endowed with the gift of lying pathetically and shamelessly and who can produce rhetoric effects almost out of anything, would have been capable of attaining such a feat. In pursuance of their common policy, for the purpose of its triumph, he had invented and organized a whole apparatus of propaganda by means of which he had built up for the nation Ion Antonescu's personality. Not as it truly is, but in the superlative, idealized. And now, the limit: Ion Antonescu, whose reason isn't up to the task, has started to wander and actually believes himself to be a saint, and the one ordained by the heavens, and he is trying to force him, the inventor of all these cock-and-bull stories, to believe in them!... How ridiculous!... How terribly ridiculous but, indeed, history has witnessed many cases of people upon whom destiny bestowed absolute powers.

With the intention of deceiving the masses and of imposing dictators upon them, the trumpeters from among their followers have described them only in superlative terms. By sustained efforts, such superlatives have successfully been imposed upon the public opinion. But unfortunately, the dictators who have been attributed these qualities have forgotten the propaganda stunt and have started to believe that they are fully deserved and that they express the truth and nothing but the truth about themselves. Today a Hitler or a Mussolini is ready to punish even those who have invented their saintly qualities if they dare question their truth.*

---

* The author recognizes that he had wrote and published these pages in the time of Ceausescu's dictatorship and, for that reason, is not sure if, in his intimacy and feelings, Marshall Antonescu arrived so far with his dictatorial mind. He asks the reader to take these words only as an "esophique" fable, as the possible pamphlet of those days against the dictatorial mentality.

Ion Antonescu hadn't even had supporters. He had had only himself. Himself and that's all. As for the rest, Valer Pop, Mares and a few others, none of which was his match, and then followed a huge gap. It had been the smallest group possible and a most obscure one, too. But it had at a given moment appeared as a necessity for certain great financial interests. Their policy had corresponded to the desire of a lot of little or big owners, commercial societies and all private enterprises who wished to be rid of both Nazi and Bolshevik populism: the iron-guards and the insincere pressing exerted by Moscow's trade union agents for the Communism represented only by some Utopian intellectuals, in a little Marxist-party not able to explain, neither for our moral and religious working-class, nor for themselves, the criminal policy of Lenin and Stalin. This on the one hand. On the other hand, their partly pro Hitler orientation was linked to those spheres of German capital which had brought Hitler to power. Viewed with lucidity, this was all the game. But can a man preserve his lucidity when within a period of less than four years - from 5 September 1940, when he appointed himself for the first time leader of the state – his glory and his renown had increased to such an extent that he had now come to be proclaimed "the Marshal", "the father of the land and of the army", "the absolute master", "the hero of the nation", "the principal pillar of the national Romanian character"?!! Frightened by the neighboring bolshevism and warned by them traditions concerning the East-Danger, The Romanians accepted the idea that this honest, faithful and austere experimented general maybe them rescuer face to the Red Danger confirmed by the military occupation of our Basarabia, through the abuses of the pact signed by Ribbentropp and Molotov!...

Well he lca, knows only too well how he made him become what he is today, for he built up this image by dint of his worth, his pen and his intelligence...

In 1940 he wrote: "God made our general out of rock and lightning."

It was also in 1941 that the said: "The entire war spirit of our ancestors resounds within our Marshal like within a voivode's horn." Furthermore, he was later to call him constantly and at every opportunity "the apostle of the nation", compelling all the propaganda services to introduce this formula into all tinted papers and paying with heavy cash, taken from secret funds which he alone had charge of, for all the press to take up this formula over and over again.

And beginning with the second anniversary of the establishment of the dictatorship, he styled him, without any scruple, "superman", drawing the country's attention to the fact that "God sent him to us at the crucial moment of the century"...

He had done all this devotedly... and, of course, prompted by his own interests, as Ion Antonescu's cause had become his own cause, too. They were not relatives. It was a mere coincidence of names. But due to Ion Antonescu he had made himself known to the high finance which through them was seeking a solution. He had fully identified himself with the dictatorship's most secret aspects and he hadn't been ashamed of using pompous words to embellish it.

Because they had had to surmount a great handicap: the tradition royalty had managed to establish for over three quarters of a century, the popularity gained by the political parties over the decades, the small but well-organized group of fanatics formed by the iron-guards. Under these circumstances, he hadn't had any alternative or even time to find the adequate words; each and every opportunity had to be used and exploited. He had uttered bombastic words, but at least he had uttered them, he had employed the most resounding epithets, but he had employed them obstinately. He had never weighed his adjectives, he had never faltered to use any attribute - the campaign had to be sustained vehemently and he, Mihai Antonescu, had sustained it, he had dedicated himself to it without bothering that he was discrediting himself and that the country laughed at him when it heard his far-fetched adulations. He had first tried to sway the iron-guards over to their side. So they both took to wearing green shirts and on the day of Saint Michael and Saint Gabriel they piously knelt down in front of their icons at the Patriarchate. Then later, as the iron-guards in their entirely illogical fanaticism had turned the slogan "Long live the legion and its captain" into their salute and password, with the politeness required not to irritate these madmen and by making an appeal to formal logics he proved to them that Zelea Codreanu - the captain — being dead, it was hardly possible for him to live long, no matter how often they might greet each other in this way. And he made the suggestion to them that they should change their password into "Long live: the legion and the general", that is Ion Antonescu who was a general at the time and the recently self-appointed head of state. It would have been a great blow, which would have grafted this general, known only in the military circles, on the ambitious stem of the iron-guards fanaticism and would have turned him into the password of fascism which was striving to strike roots in Romania...

But he hadn't succeeded. Even his insinuating and skillful pleading had failed this time. Quite on the contrary, not long after, the iron-guards organized a rebellion which decreed that "Ion Antonescu is a historical calamity, as he has done at least as much harm to the country as King Carol II."

After discharging Horia Sima from the government, Ion Antonescu had the army suppress the iron-guards rebellion. For

Mihai Antonescu, this had been the favor- able moment for taking over the office of Deputy Premier within the Council of Ministers, office which had been imposed by the iron-guards, and vacant now, as he professed a policy more intelligently linked to certain interests of Romanian capital.

    Thus he, Mihai Antonescu, with his lucrative and enterprising brain had had to exist on earth for the purpose of making propaganda for the insignificantly notorious personality of the Marshal when he had remained all alone on the platform and was no longs backed by the iron-guards who had previously been the political basis of the regime. Through his articles, speeches, conferences and slogans he had made him known to the country. Through Orders of the Day, songs and prayers he had made him more well-known and well-respected in the army. He had made him popular in the churches by means of sermons and the phrase "We are still praying for our Marshall ruler of the State". But above all, he had made him popular with that stratum of the bourgeoisie which was directly interested in not having anything to do with the extremists, that bourgeoisie which didn't wish to' be threatened either by fascism or by communism. The Marshal, previously a perfect military man but unknown in politics, who had been brought to power by a favorable concurrence of circumstances and not by any special previous social-political merit of his own, had become the buffer man of these conservative aspirations. His present dictatorship, after setting the country free from the aegis of the Iron-Guard, firmly directed the Army, protected the active population more or less wealthy from both the rebellions of the Right and the revolution of the Left. It was for this social category, which had every reason to back him, that Mihai Antonescu had advised the Marshal to declare on 6 November 1941, in the proclamation for the plebiscite by which he asked for the nation's vote of confidence: "The new Romanian state must devote all its efforts towards the formation and strengthening of our bourgeoisie ..." And thus, from a commonplace officer, he had become the man of the moment. But what he had become was due to him, and this is the reason for Mihai Antonescu's resentment. Because he was the one who had placed on his commonplace forehead of a narrow-minded man the aura of the nation's apostle who embodied everybody's rightfully cherished dream: the reunifying of the country. Therefore, through his ability, he had raised the Marshal to the platform of national concern and had put the king and the Royal House into the shade.

Mrs. Maria Antonescu had become also a leading public figure in the nation's life thanks to the role she played in the Council of Patronage which had been devised by Ica to this end and which made of her the mother of the wounded, the soother of wounds, the benefactress of the orphans and of the widows. He had thus enabled her to perform the most melodramatic role in front of the public opinion, also dealing yet another blow to royalty by definitely pushing aside the nondescript person of Queen-mother Helen.

And thus, out of the Marshal and his wife, Mihai Antonescu had created the country's future reigning family, trying to completely wipe out the very purpose of the Royal House. It is not as blameless a family as it is said to be, for the Marshal's scrupulous correctness is annihilated by Maria Antonescu's dark dealings made through the Council of Patronage. But Ica's duty is to polish up this aura more and more, paving the way for tomorrow's reigning family whose heir, firstly from the spiritual point of view but also through the resemblance of name, was he. In his innermost ambitions, this is what Mihai Antonescu is dreaming to become. But in everyday life he confines himself to be, for the moment, the Marshal's Vice-President, Minister of Foreign Affairs and Minister of Propaganda.

He is satisfied with his status. Or to be more accurate, he used to be satisfied with it. Until he came to understand that everything he had built up for the Marshal as a mask for the opinion of the man in the street, everything he had added to the banal personality of the ordinary man to turn his guise into a voievod commemorative fresco for the nation, that all the heraldic symbols he had invented for him and the image of a saint which he had painted had become things which the Marshal had started to believe in. In consequence of his megalomania, he had stopped thinking that he is only the hazardous invention of those patriotic and influential interests which, in a moment of acute crisis, needed the dictatorship of a devoted officer. And so, the Marshall has started to believe himself to be an apostle.

But he too, Mihai Antonescu, is a megalomaniac. He knows how to put on airs, he is skillful in assuming guises and in obtaining undeserved praises, he excels in feigning to be a great intellectual and an unequalled patriot. But in his heart of hearts he has always preserved a sense of the great riskiness of this game. He is content that his affectations are working out so well, but he does not delude himself by believing in what he has made others believe. Underneath his beige silk shirts and fine clothes, elegantly tailored, he knows exactly how much he is worth and he is proud only of one thing: that he has a gift for fooling everybody and for playing much more important roles than objective reality would enable him to. But he performs his part with a certain amount of rationality and caution, paying great attention to the social category he is in duty bound to serve. Moreover, he is quite conscious of and always bears in mind his future situation, calculating his every move carefully and weighing the measure of possible exaggeration when faced with human stupidity and servility, invariably extorting all virtual advantages. He has, however, also an eye on the lower step just behind him, his forces ready to descend to it with lucidity, to rally as it were, to take all the necessary safety measures for the moment when he might run up against hardships. This is what he calls up-dated rational policy: to impose oneself upon others without any scruples and to take on all possible guises; all that counts is that things should work out to one's advantage. But one must always remain aware of one's actual value. This is the only way one can experience the great satisfaction of pulling everybody's legs...

On the runway, the Forces General Staff Commander's plane is landing and Mihai Antonescu, pondering over his efforts for his chief political situation and his own rescue from this trouble, break off his impulsive thinks and, with a loving smile prepare his welcome. To encourage the Marshall, he is in readiness to give him information confirming that Romania keep its more independent status than in other countries dominated by Hitler's troops and the occidental emissaries parachuted are protected from the SS and able to transmit our government's armistice messages. But, to calm his master, he will don't underline that, proving a firm geopolitical protocol among the Big Powers, the last answers to these messages oblige us to pay attention only to the Moscow's accept.

....

XL

Bucharest is blacked out entirely. The policemen fine people for the faint shafts of light which escape under the window-frames. Or they close their eyes when bribed as if, once bribed, the enemy air force could no longer discover the places where to drop their bombs. But they know that, at this time of night, they can be sure of promptly receiving a tip, because in eight out of ten cases, the people are listening in to London, Moscow, or the Voice of America on their radios. Thus the good fortune of the Romanian policeman, generally recruited from among that despicable category of people who hope to shirk the obligation of working, hips him to take his clandestine gift and enables him to have money to pay for a glass or two of plum-brandy, just like his chiefs who, belonging to a higher social category, are consequently more fastidious and take their bribes from the notorious delinquents, making therefore enough money to buy themselves houses, gardens, cars. And indeed, at this very hour, their higher chief, the Undersecretary of State and Minister, General Piki Vasiliu, is making the inventory of the amount he has managed to put aside, he is calculating how much he should leave to his wife and what he should take for himself and his mistress from Caransebes in order to spend the rest of their days abroad. Then he puts everything into his car and, taking advantage of the black-out which screens and conceals all his movements, he drives all his suitcases and bags to the Stefan cel Mare highroad where he carries them into the building decked with towers and brick battlements and look-outs, a building which is the headquarters of the military police. With its camouflaged windows, the edifice is blind and only the summons of the sergeant on duty disturbs the darkness: "Halt, give the password!" To which the officer' who is the general's aide and confidant at the same time, bending under the weight of the luggage, gives the answer: "Damn you! ... You bloody ass, it's his Excellency, the Minister!" And with these words, without rousing the slightest suspicion, they enter the building wherefrom the guarding of the country is directed, carrying the most eloquent of all corpus delicti - the luggage with which, within twenty-four hours, the minister in charge of the country's peace and order is to run away across the frontiers. As in all critical situations, the best hiding place is the most exposed one, a place nobody would ever have dreamed of controlling.

Let us take for instance this massive, stately building, erected as if to enhance the ruthless gravity of the repressive apparatus whose commander it is at present offering cover to. Who could ever deem that an evil-doer might even dare approach it, knowing that he would be caught and arrested in a trice. But since in this first half of the twentieth century the notion of law is still very lax, so it is with evil-doers too. Just like in the classical instances when only prigs go to jail while the great thieves and robbers are styled magnates and are regarded as the pillars of society. And now let us see what a blacked-out night can conceal in this unique building of Bucharest. In an out-of-the-way wing of the edifice, well-guarded and provided with a certain degree of comfort, are the roams confining the three British officers who were parachuted with a transmitter radio station on to Romanian territory. Although only one of them is of Romanian origin - his name being Metianu - the most important connections in Romania are held by an Englishman who has, as a matter of fact, been sent to Romania as the head of their small group. He is Chastelaine, former director of a Romanian-British oil enterprise at Ploiesti. Having become the chief of the Intelligence Service for the Balkan area, with its headquarters in Istanbul, he had had Romania in his charge over the entire period of the war. Together with his two companions and an emission-reception radio-set and also a map of paramount importance, he was parachuted in the surroundings of Bucharest on Christmas. The map contained all the data concerning the attempts of negotiating a peace agreement between the representatives of Hitler and the Great Powers and it pointed out all the territorial conditions debated upon. It demonstrated that in the event of signing a treaty with the Soviet Union, Ion Antonescu's great ally, Adolf Hitler, after having drained Romania of all its resources and cannon-fodder, did not deign to consider it in a future configuration of Europe. This map was to be conveyed to Ion Antonescu with a view to drawing his attention to the sort of ally he was being loyal to.

Under the circumstances, on New Year's Eve, Ion Antonescu sent H. Giorgie-Barbul as his emissary to Stockholm in order to confer with the counselor of the Soviet Union Embassy in Sweden. H. Giorgie-Barbul returned with armistice conditions for Romania which revealed the concern of the Red Army to be rid of the resistance put up along the alignment of a front in this country. However, Ion Antonescu continued to remain loyal to Hitler who completely overlooked the Marshal in his negotiations regarding a possible peace. In exchange, the three emissaries have remained under a severe guard in this wing of the General Inspectorate of the Military Police although the Gestapo has repeatedly demanded that they be handed over to them. At this moment, Cristescu, chief of Antonescu's Intelligence Service has just finished paying a visit to the latter. Accompanied by Major Unga, the officer who has been assigned to attend to the instruction and care of these three highly significant detainees, he endeavors to give the impression that he has been on one of his usual routine visits. The major, of course, feigns to believe him and salutes respectfully while slamming the door of the car which has been waiting outside in the pitch darkness of the street... Cristescu heads for the Presidency of the Council of Ministers, a building lying in the neighborhood so that he may witness the Marshal's reception of Dr. Clodius, Hitler's special envoy. But this, however, only after he has assured himself of his being able to send one of the British prisoners as a messenger to the Allies in case of need.

The office of the Undersecretary of State who also holds the function of Commander General Inspector of the Military Police Force is on the first floor of the building. Inside, Piki Vasiliu establishes with his right-hand man the data of the postponed flight, the means of loading all the luggage into the plane and his meeting his other aide who, the next day, is to bring the lady from Caransebes and finally, the way he, General Vasiliu, is to arrive in the nick of time before the plane is ready to take off. Thereafter, the general makes another control phone-call to Caransebes, to convince himself that the lady, all her jewels and foreign bills are prepared to be carried into the car, pursuant to their setting out the next day at dawn as early as possible for

Bucharest. He admonishes his mistress telling her that it is only for her sake that he is putting off their departure for another day, although everything was arranged for their leaving this night. She must understand that for a man who has decided to leave on what is not just an ordinary trip but a giving up of a situation, for a man who has set the exact date for this exploit, it is very difficult to wait, that in this case the so-called "Reisefieber" gnaws at one's hart. He implores her to start out at the break of day so as to arrive in Bucharest the next day in the evening. Then they will order their last dinner in the red private salon at Capsa Restaurant, after which they will ultimately take off. And as her voice with sweet Transylvanian accent on the vowels has a calming effect on his nervous system, he sits down at his desk and prepares himself thoroughly for the next day's session of the Council of Ministers. At the hour when the session was to open, he had planned to be far away in same country with a different religion: Turkey or, if the plane flew smoothly, even Egypt. But in the present circumstances, he will have the pleasure of seeing the Marshal once again, his friend of early youth to whom, being two years his senior, he had been to a certain extent instructor at the military school... He will sacrifice himself and put up with him tomorrow once again. But, as for the day after tomorrow, nothing will be able to stop him from taking a walk with his mistress among muezzins, minarets and Allied troops. And from there on he is to return to Christian soil, to Spain where his friend, Pamfil Seicaru is expecting him.

On the second floor of the building there are two equally sumptuous offices belonging to the Deputy Commander, General Tobescu, and to the Chief of the General Staff, General Anton. Both are at their duty and only the blacked-out windows make them undistinguishable in the dark night for the man in the street. General Tobescu does not leave his office because he has long considered himself rightfully entitled to be the Commander of the Military Police. He is older and has the most numerous years of service. His reckonings are quite simple: Piki Vasiliu is Antonescu's most intimate and most trustworthy assistant; Dumitru Popescu-Codita, Minister of Home Affairs, is a fastidious and nondescript character; in the present difficult conditions, it is more than certain that he will be replaced by Piki. Hence the conclusion: General Tobescu must not for a single moment lose control of the situation; he has all the chances to become Minister Undersecretary of State and General Commander of the Military Police Forces.

In the adjacent office, General Anton is making completely different calculations. He is one of the officers who has been brought to the side of the patriotic movement. Having been informed by Colonel Damaceanu, he has accepted to put himself at the disposal and under the orders of the men preparing the insurrection. Now, he is making the necessary preparations for the entry into disposition of the five thousand military policemen he has under his command in the capital with a view to their ensuring the further functioning of the main state institutions and the preventing of any German attack.

He recalls how, several weeks ago, Colonel Damaceanu announced himself at his office', how he came in and how, while talking, he preserved an unusual stiffness in his military protocol bearing. They were old acquaintances, almost friends, and that is why his behavior was the more embarrassing. Until at last, Damaceanu, unable to hold himself back any longer, told him bluntly: "I know that you can have me arrested on the spot and that from here I might never see the sun till the day of my execution. But my mission is to propose to you to pass over to the side of those who want to overthrow Antonescu..." The Chief of the General Staff of the Military Police thought the matter over for a while: it did not seem to be a provocation and, coming from such a man, it couldn't be any such thing.

Everything unfolded briefly, like between army men, men who know very well how to take quick decisions. Colonel Damaceanu was risking never leaving the place at all of leaving it after having gained a new ally to his side. There were no two ways about it; he did however succeed in the latter.

Three offices within the same massive building with threatening corridors. Three career officers, commanders of the repressive apparatus. Three entirely different perspectives. But seen from the street, the night and the camouflage make this building appear as looming and as silent as a rock. .

....

A summer evening in Bucharest: news carried by the evening newspapers, which seem to be ignorant of the putsch ready to break out, and conspirator aspects of the movement. Clandestine printing houses are however preparing the publications which will announce the overthrow.

XLV

Motioning politely to Dr. Clodius to sit down for the second interview of that evening, the Marshal looks Mihai Antonescu in the eyes to apprehend if the latter has thoroughly gone into matters with Hitler's envoy. Ica's glance is more telling than are the words uttered in his habitual affected tone: "Dr. Clodius and myself have had a wide-ranging exchange of opinions as regards the situation that would occur if Turkey accepted to offer bases for the Allied air force, and we have also lengthily debated on the matter of our economic obligations for the present month to the Reich..."

Ion Antonescu nods in agreement towards the German plenipotentiary, promising that he will presently corroborate the content of their discussions and begs them to pardon him for a moment. He exits into the anteroom, he crosses it passing by the petrified officers, he opens the door of a small-sized office at the far end of the room and at one glance grasps the meaning of the answer conveyed to him by his principal secretary, Colonel Romeo Zaharia, and orders that General Pantazi, the Minister of War, be summoned to his presence, he carefully opens another door leading into the tiny salon where Eugen Cristescu, the chief of his Intelligence Service, interminably drawing with a sharp tipped pencil delicate filigrees on a sheet of paper, is waiting for him in the attitude of a man accustomed to waiting infinitely. Antonescu on the run, blurts out not even giving him time to salute: "Take somebody along with you, a trustworthy jurist or a military magistrate, and go over to Mr. Maniu. You will inform him officially: <Marshal Antonescu is offering you the Premiership of the State with a view to your immediately concluding the armistice, he also begs you to write him your answer... That's all. Tomorrow you will come to my office with his answer in writing!"...

Cristescu, miming indifference, says with precision: "At this time of day he must be with Bratianu, later he will go to the Palace". Antonescu decides: "Well, all right, you will bring me the answer tomorrow."

And, while Cristescu discreetly leaves the room by another door, the Marshal returns reassured and relaxed to Dr. Clodius. He is extremely content with his decision of having asked Maniu to give an answer in writing: "In this way he won't be able to retract later... He takes the Premiership, he's welcome to it. But, what if he turns it down?"... While turning these thoughts over in his mind, he re-enters his roomy office where he finds that General Pantazi, the Minister of War, has, arrived too. He addresses Dr. Clodius directly: "I trust that Mr Mihai Antonescu has acquainted you with my intention of withdrawing from the war... Yes, Doctor, I must withdraw and, as a loyal ally, I ask for the assent of Germany."

Dr. Clodius is quite taken aback. He has just come from Turkey. From Turkey where Hitler had sent him on a mission to persuade president Inonu not to give air force bases to the Allies. And Inonu had in no way given him any hope that he would satisfy the entreaty. All he had told him was that for the meanwhile the Turkish government had not taken any decision in this respect... That was all he had told him and he, Clodius, on his way back to Germany, had stopped in Romania just for the sake of not returning to Hitler empty-handed. He had stopped only to establish what economic goods would be delivered by Romania to Germany in the present month, in keeping with the demands put forward by Hitler on his 5 August meeting with Antonescu. And now, instead of returning to Germany with several trains of tank-cars full of petrol and a harvest of grain and the fruits of this early autumn, instead of being able to see Hitler growing merry on it being reported to him that, thanks to the economic policy carried out by Dr. Clodius in Romania, the German soldier's rations were being maintained at a high level, here he was being compelled to become the bearer of the most unfortunate news. He would have better not stopped in Bucharest. Nobody had obliged him to come here. He had been sent on a special mission to Ankara and only an ill-fated inspiration had made him decide in the last moment not to by-pass Bucharest!...

In his account, Antonescu is willing to go into details about everything. It is, in fact, quite obvious that he has prepared himself specially for this purpose. Also, it is for the first time in their consultations, in which they have always discussed the top-secret problems of the Romanian-German collaboration, that the Marshal has summoned General Pantazi to their presence. General Pantazi, who proves to be very well-informed, is reporting on the entire situation on the front. By acquiring the attitude of a crossexaminer, Antonescu asks him terse questions thus obliging the general to give a most accurate description of the highly critical situation of both the Romanian troops and of the German Southern Ukraine Army Group. He goes on and on, despite the fact that the German minister makes resigned gestures to the effect that he fully trusts the Romanian Marshal's assertions. Antonescu expounds his reasons over and over again, naturally, from the need of a person justifying his action. He wants Hitler's assent. But Clodius's dream of obtaining trains with tank-cars of petrol, and freight-cars of grain and fresh fruit and vegetables has long since vanished. In its place has appeared the image of Hitler seized by a fit of fury after having hard the grimmest news he, Clodius, could have brought to him. For, evidently, - he has after all just come from Turkey which has been neutral so far - Ion Antonescu is Hitler's last reliable ally.

The Marshal keeps speaking. After having described the battlefront, he specifies that he, as a matter of fact, warned Friessner the day before yesterday that if he did not get another German division of armored cars on the Moldavian front. he deemed he was entitled to take full liberty of action. And the fact is that he has received no answer to this request of his from the German OKW. Therefore, it stands to reason that he is entitled to take liberty of action. But he will not. He will first discharge his duty of an upright military man by first asking for the assent of his allies.

Overwhelmed by the news as such, Dr. Clodius needs no further arguments. For him the arguments are redundant. But Antonescu fails to apprehend this. He is set on giving his reasons and once he has started, he will see it through: "The Bulgarian Prime Minister publicly stated that everything that had been done previously, that is all their collaboration with Hitler was a mistake and he added that now they were waiting for the assistance of their

Slav brother; in Montenegro, Tito has launched a big counter-offensive; Turkey has severed relations with Germany and has ceased its delivery of meat, it has also closed up the Dardanelles and it will most certainly offer air force bases to the Allies; and all that coupled with the Russian offensive which is unfolding vigorously" with unprecedented might"… So it is up to him, Antonescu, to take a swift decision.

Just to do his duty, Clodius reminds him that the news of tonight concerning the offensive is much more encouraging. The German troops have rallied and have put up a firm resistance halting the Soviet advance. The Romanian troops, naturally, under the command of his, the Marshal's, military skill have also seized more stable positions and have overcome the moment of rout. And then, an offensive is always vigorous in its first days. It depends on how it is put a stop to. And, the telephone conversation he had just now with the commander of the Southern Ukraine troops, right here from the Marshal's office, has confirmed that the situation may be changed for the better during the coming night.

Dr. Clodius offers this report only to discharge his duty. For he senses the unwavering determination of this short, stubborn military man.

Antonescu too is well-informed. Yes, he knows the situation has improved at the front. And he also knows it can be further improved. His estimates, and he is not being subjective for they have been confirmed by General Pantazi and the entire General Staff, show that if he checks the offensive, he can hold out several months. But he wants to use this situation not to fight but to save of Romania that territory which has not as yet been crossed into by the Russians. It is for this reason that now, during these ensuing favorable days of reversal of the tide on the front he would like to have consultations with the Soviets concerning the conditions of the armistice. Because he would like to impose certain conditions, not just accept any terms like a vanquished army does.

Having made this demonstration, perhaps for his own sake too, Ion Antonescu draws up to Hitler's minister and says with conviction: "Herr Doktor, I have observed you have been understanding, attentive and receptive to my arguments. I am a soldier who knows how to appraise his combat forces exactly. Well, I shall not conceal it from you that I can still fight and hold out for quite a time yet. As an ally who has behaved frankly, I request a favor of Germany: let it authorize me to withdraw from the war now when, having held up the Russian offensive, I can impose certain conditions. That is all I have to say, Herr Doktor, I want to get an answer from Germany to the effect that it authorizes me to withdraw from the war."

Rising to his feet, Dr. Clodius confirms the fact that he understands the situation all too well, that the Marshal's arguments are fully grounded and that they cannot but be taken into account. He speaks slowly, choosing his words carefully, pointing to the fact that he had indeed been considering the words he has just listened to. But at the same time, the guise of an understanding man which he has assumed might just as well be a diplomatic maneuver to gain time and not to alert Antonescu's supporters with an openly declared opposition and to create for himself a respite to inform Hitler, to wait for the results of the next day's counter-offensive in order to see if Rastenburg doesn't somehow issue a command for Romania to be completely occupied by German troops. In any case, his attitude is one of apparent understanding. He makes known his intention of staying in Romania on the next day too, and he asks the Marshal to set him an appointment for the afternoon, so as to be able to talk things over when they are in possession of more accurate data.

This suits Antonescu too, for he is awaiting an answer from Germany. He, therefore, sets the appointment with military precision for the same place the following day, 23 August, at 5.30 p.m.

Clodius confirms that he will come to this same office on 23 August at 5.30 p.m. and leaves for Snagov, to the villa of a German brewer by the name Czell, a villa at which he invariably puts up whenever he comes to Bucharest. Alone in the car racing towards Snagov, he once again curses the ill-fated moment when he decided to come over to Romania without anyone having requested it of him.

In exchange, Ion Antonescu, dressed after the military English fashion in his uniform with lighter colored trousers, is most active in his office on the second floor of the building housing the Council of Ministers. Together with Mihai Antonescu he is drafting a message to General Wilson, the Commander in Chief of the Allied Forces in the Near East and East Mediterranean. A major message in which he, Ion Antonescu, announces him that he is willing to conclude the armistice and, as an army man addressing another army man, he conveys to him the entreaty to assist him in obtaining reasonable and, within measure, advantageous conditions of armistice for Romania.

XLVI

Patrascanu had been driven to the Palace, as he usually was, by Ionescu Balaceanu, a civil servant working in the office of the Marshal of the Palace and the confidential person of the young men who had coalesced round the king. Known to the commander of the guards, the car would enter by the palace gate without being checked and it would pull up along one of the back alleys in front of the service entrances. From there, Patrascanu would be led along discreet corridors lest he should be seen and recognized either by one of the security agents accredited to the king's retinue of by some security man secretly appointed to soma, service in the palace. He would be led discreetly and cautiously to the middle of the park where, surrounded only by his own confidential people, the king lived in a newly-built house.

Things had taken place in the same way the previous evening, only that they had been conducted somewhat more swiftly. The king wanted to see him as fast as possible so that they might exchange views before Maniu's arrival. And, indeed, as soon as he entered the room, Mihai, smoking rather nervously, pulled him aside to a corner of his study and informed him that almost all the details concerning the overthrow were ready, the only thing remaining was the necessity of convincing Maniu to become the Premier of the new government. In view of this fact, he, the king, asked Patrascanu to accept the cabinet formula that would be conditioned by Maniu, thus making him accept the Premiership and rendering him incapable of putting things off any longer.

Patrascanu now understood why the king had hastened him to his presence to exchange a few opinions with him: it was naturally an allusion to the fact that he had always required the portfolio of Justice for the Communists. He answered condescendingly that he had heard of certain negotiation between the National Peasant Party and the National Liberal Party regarding the fact that Maniu wished to cede the Ministry of Justice to the Liberals in exchange for the Ministry of Economy and he added that, as concerns the Ministry of Justice, the Communists had claims of content and not of form towards it. Then he asked the king whether he was convinced that Maniu, even though his demands were granted, would accept the Premiership. The king shrugged his shoulders and said: "We are in duty bound to do our utmost"... Patrascanu confirmed that he too, considered the government should be headed by a well-known personality like Mr Maniu and that therefore he would, to the best of his ability, try to persuade him to accept the office. He also said that it was normal, as they had agreed previously, that the cabinet should be presided by a politician who enjoyed authority both in the country and abroad, and the only impediment seemed to be Mr. Maniu's hesitation in accepting the assignment.

At that moment, Mr. Maniu accompanied by Mr. Bratianu arrived and the king, impatient, opened the interview inquiring whether they had brought along with them their proposals for the future government. The two aged men exchanged glances as if they did not understand what it was all about. After some time, Maniu drawled solemnly: "We shall bring them along tomorrow, rest assured, Your Majesty, we will bring them along!" And, as a justification which was completely redundant in the context of the pervading general hypocrisy, he added: "We still have a few things to talk over, to weigh... some estimates to be worked out"...

On hearing these words, Patrascanu ejaculated: "Mr Maniu, you have been promising to give us the list of your cabinet since Visoianu left for Cairo. You keep promising you will give it, but you never do! Why are you forever putting things off in this way? Do you intend to postpone matters sine die?!"... And turning towards the king he uttered firmly: "Your Majesty, I think it is high time you acted more resolutely. This has been going on not only since Visoianu left several months ago, but now, recently, since last week I have been meeting Mr. Maniu every evening and I have been given one and same answer every time: 'tomorrow'.

You will have to resort to Your Majesty's authority and oblige these gentlemen to draw up the list of the cabinet right now !"

On hearing these imperative sentences, Maniu, surprised, riveted his exophthalmic eyes upon Patrascanu's face with an expression of candor as though wishing to ask: "What on earth has come over you my good man?" Then he became grave and repressed a cough which would have cleared his throat had he had the intention of answering. But his tactics was invariably to keep silent: "the less one speaks, the fewer commitments one has." He therefore acquired an annoyed mien and sank into a somber sphinxlike silence.

Patrascanu, attributing to himself more liberties of action than have the Moscow's subordinates, received no answer from Maniu but he did get one from Niculescu-Buzesti, a young, outstanding member of the National Peasant Party, a most acid and intelligent man who was playing a triple game: a National Peasant Party front-ranker, a Mihai Antonescu's head of the policy-management department in the Ministry of Foreign Affairs, where of late he had even been allowed to endorse the ministerial duties of ad-interim when Ica keeps the place of Prime minister, and, alongside Mocioni-Stircea, Ioanitiu and General Sanatescu, a member of the group closest to the king.

Happy to be able to assert himself by parrying the words addressed to the leader of his party, Grigore Niculescu-Buzesti accused Patrascanu: "It is not Mr Maniu's fault but yours; for it is you who will insist on having the Ministry of Justice that is why you cannot arrive at an agreement!"

Quick-tempered and determined to settle matters that evening, an evening which was only five days away from the date established for the overthrow of the dictatorship, Lucretiu Patrascanu flared up. He reminded them of all their protractions since June to the present moment, he reminded them that the day of reckoning was approaching, and that they would have to account for the spokes they had tried to put in the wheel of progress. He had declared itself in favor of a government presided over by Mr Maniu, but he, Mr Maniu kept refusing and suffered himself to be begged too much. And as to the Ministry of Justice, it was not an ambition of the Communists represented by him (Patrascanu don't tells how), but a necessity; it was the guarantee that all the antifascist militants would be set free directly. Their immediate liberation could be wholly secured only with him holding the portfolio of Justice.

Patrascanu's authoritative tone determined the king to intervene in the dispute. He sensed the danger. He felt it in his bones that they would come to threats because, encouraged by them political opportunity, the Communists were driving a hard bargain, and he wanted to take the sting out of things and to restore harmony. This huge, burning wish of his to compose the differences among themselves worked a miracle: the king, this stodgy, stammering youth, still wearing the clothes he had been dressed in when he left Sinaia - a whitish wind jacket and rather baggy trousers - became for a few moments a genuine orator and politician speaking and, especially, thinking in terms of such fluency and persuasion that when the interview was over, Patrascanu overheard Niculescu-Buzesti saying to Baron Stircea: "It is noticeable that you have been instructing him."

That was a matter that could not be known for sure. But fact is that this young man felt he could no longer remain a puppet; he knew by instinct that the Palace was in danger and that he was called upon to do something for the royal institution he represented. This obliged him both to think more responsibly and to become more competent than he appeared to be in reality. And, surrounded by experienced statesmen who were nevertheless acting to their own advantage and were thus postponing the settlement of things, he had proved to be highly realistic and practical. He said bluntly: "I don't understand why you cling to a fetish and keep putting decisions off, Mr Maniu. The formula for the cabinet is transitory. It is not a given fact which cannot be changed and cannot be amended if needs he. Cabinet reshuffles have sometimes been operated from one day to another. Therefore your arguments that things must be thought over and weighed are not grounded and it means you look upon me as being a child if you consider I ought to believe them." Then, turning towards Patrascanu who was exulted: "And you, Mr Patrascanu, who are the extreme representative in matters of democracy, should observe the principles of democracy to a higher extent!" - he said admonishingly hinting to him that in his claims he was one against three. Then, for a few moments he truly became the king, head of the House of Hohenzollern, applying his mind to the interests of his throne and mediating between the politicians: "Please do understand me; I have come to realize that I must urge you to take action. And I must be vigilant lest we should get entangled in our own threads. Do you think that I am not aware of what the persons hesitating to get involved and preferring a royal cabinet are after?... In the event of peace bringing in its wake heavy and humiliating conditions for the country, they would prefer a royal government rather than themselves to take the responsibility in the face of history, yes, that's what they would like! You want royalty to be held responsible and not yourselves, yes, that's the truth of the matter, gentlemen!"...

His youthful face showed sincere indignation. He had in fact picked out the real point at issue. Patrascanu was sensible of his state of mind and he answered with the same sincerity: "Under these conditions and circumstances, the common interests are obliging all the political parties to assume the responsibility of the document, and I solemnly state here!"..."You, indeed; but your comrades?" – insinuates Niculescu-Buzesti something concerning the internal fight among the Communists. But Patrascanu is full of sincerity: "In this moment I have a self-interest: to set them free of the camps and prisons before to be assassinated by SS!"...

The moment was heavy and grave. The yellow room in the New House was charged with a dense and menacing silence mingled with the misty clouds of cigarette smoke which were floating about in bluish-yellow streaks. With its yellow silk-lined walls and its heavy mahogany furniture, carved along lines which although observing the century-old styles introduced a touch of elegant modernism, the yellow room had become the audience room since the king had moved into the New House standing in the middle of the park. It had never as yet witnessed such a solemn moment. The king, a carelessly dressed young man, with big hands much more skilled in mechanics and a stammering manner of speech which was most inappropriate for oratory, had come to lucidly understand the game and its imperatives. His concern to maintain the institution represented by royalty, led him, more than it did the experienced statesmen, to the need of taking the decisions and actions demanded by the moment. Understanding him and appreciating his sincere gesture, Patrascanu suffered himself to be most sincere too, drawing everybody's attention to the actual state of affairs: "Yes, it is a common interest we share, Your Majesty, let us make these gentlemen understand that!... And, continuing his unexpected sincerity, he answers to Buzesti: " You asked about my comrades. You have reason; maybe they will prosecute me for this political compromise made by myself, don't agreeing to wait for the Red Army occupation. But now, I have a self-target: To save as minister the convicts which I wasn't able to save like barrister"... Usually rational, lucid and restrained, conscientious to play a big card, he is troubled by an impulsive refuse to accept the politicians mean hesitations and, haunted by sincerity, warn the: "Yes, gentlemen, both I and other comrades of mine may one day be asked why we made a compact with you instead of overthrowing you as the laws of the revolution require. Mark my words, gentlemen, some time, in the future, somebody might accuse me for having cooperated with you! Some person or other may say that I abandoned the firmness of revolutionary principles and even persuade a lot of people to have me punished severely for my having played into your hands. But I am not playing into your hands, I am a democrat and I am responding to the country's pressing need to rally all the forces that can ensure the overthrow of the dictatorship and bring democracy to power. I openly state here that I am not interested in becoming Minister of Justice, but I am interested in being positively sure that the very instant after the launching of the insurrection I shall be able to issue the decrees by which all the fighters for progress detained in prisons and concentration camps will be set free and by which democracy may flourish. Look, I solemnly state here that I accept any proposition made by Mr. Iuliu Maniu, Mr. Bratianu or Mr. Constantin-Titel Petrescu concerning any formula of a cabinet, provided that it will warrant the absolute security of all the detained democrats and their immediate liberation and will also ensure that kind of legislation which will instantly free the country!"...

....

In this moment we become known that Lucretiu Patrascanu, the self well known communist real thinker in Romania, has only some devoted friends, intellectuals which, nine years later will be prosecuted with him: Belu, Torosian, Stefan

Popescu, and Gheorghe Dinu. Now, they are preparing a secret number for a newspaper to be distributed in the firsts hours of liberty with them appeal and the decrees to liberate the political prisoners.

Patrascanu is supported also by some present prisoners whose trials he has defended, but never by the agents introduced by Moscow.

Known as a left-public-personality before the war, son of a writer Member of Parliament, he has stable connections with the Palace, collaborating with Titulescu and Dr. Lupu when these ones established diplomatic relations with Litvinov. In present, also, he have the recommendation and the guarantee of his relative, the colonel Octav Ullea, Governor of the Palace's Ceremonial, of the opponents of Antonescu's generals Mihail, Aldea and Vasiliu-Rascanu and also of the king's mentor Mocioni-Stircea, often meet in his sister's house of the Kiseleff Avenue.

He is continuing his high political relations accepted by the Palace and other parties, thanks to the geopolitical situation and the occidental conventional obligation to give priority to the communism in this part of the world, as the Great Powers established at Yalta and by other protocols. But, in fact, another group, organized only like a Soviet-provoker agency with roots in the Stalin's Third Communist International, acts on the Soviet territory by Ana Pauker, Vasile Luca, Teohari Georgescu Walter Roman, Petre Borila and some generals in the Soviet Army's captivity. In Bucharest, never like members of a party, but surely like a spying team, are in this connection Constantin Parvulescu, Emil Bodnaras and Iozef Ranghetz.

Firstly, they told to Patrascanu that he is involved as a member of the leadership of a "National Revolutionary Committee" but, after it, Patrascanu heard that the first task of this so-called "Committee" is to kill the last elected Secretary General of this party, Stefan Foris.

As a lawman, Patrascanu told them that, statutory speaking, it seems to be a wrecker-deviation and a treason of a sectary group against the internal democracy of the party. Discreetly, without commentaries, they isolated him and auctioned selves against Foris.

So Patrascanu rested self in his relations with the other parties' people. From time to time he was obliged to take as his assistant a former trade-unions worker named Constantin Hagiu who, at his turn, was informing one of the three agents with bureaucratic but no high connections in Moscow.

In parallels, a former deserter officer, Emil Bodnaras or Bodnarenco, comparatively nicknamed engineer Ceausu, organized a little commando-group in Bucharest letting know the Palace, trough the agency of the colonel Damaceanu, chief of the capital-city armies' general staff, that he is able to concentrate any worker forces. At some important interparty meetings, instead of the Hagiu's "assistance", Patrascanu was finding oneself with this man, in spite of his knowledge that Bodnaras is a member of the PCUS - Soviet Communist Bolshevik Party ,and not of the PCR - Communist Party of Romania.

....

XLVIII

The atmosphere in Ion Antonescu's office is tranquil and silent. It is for the first time so during this day which is drawing to its end. At this moment the Marshal's haggard face, stubbornly frowning to conceal his exhaustion, brightens up all of a sudden. He himself comes towards the door and a affectionately clutches General Sanatescu's long tapering hand. And with a certain degree of humor in his voice - a seldom occurrence with him – he says: "I know you're bringing me messages from that stuttering callow youth who is plotting against me, but as they are conveyed by you, I am, in any case, glad to see you."

In a dark blue suit, faultlessly tailored, which he invariably wears when he is on any conspiratorial mission, the general smiles and winks at him mischievously, as they used to do at the military cavalry school whenever they passed an examination with flying colors. "Is it bad on the front?" he asks him. Antonescu gives no direct answer. He speaks only of what he is bent on doing: I have ordained that the order of retreat from the Focsani-Namoloasa-Galatzi frontline be drafted. Tomorrow I am going to discuss these measures in the Council of Ministers and next week I shall personally be going to command the battlefront. It is a most difficult moment, Matache, believe me it is!"...

The wave of affection seems to have worn off. The former schoolboys are now two stiff elderly men studying and attempting to fathom each other at this late hour of night. "Of course it is a difficult moment", he says, "I know you feel the need to talk things over. That's why I dropped in to settle when we shall have a lengthier talk. Well, the king has asked you to come over to the palace. You have been on the front; we await your visit at any time you wish, so that you might inform us what the situation is. The king would like to know..."

Antonescu grows ever redder in the face. He answers dryly and abruptly with his mien of evil elegance, a mien which he but once dropped, three weeks earlier, in Hitler's bunker; "Let the king attend to his studies, for even so he's a dunce! I have given him the best professor in Roman and international law; I have given him Ica. Under this pretext Ica comes to the palace two or three times a week and is given the opportunity to undermine me together with those unfledged fellows; what more do you want?!" Refined Sanatescu's long narrow countenance expresses through its features a sense of gravity. His gestures are calm and of inborn decorousness. While the two deep-cut wrinkles in his cheeks grow even deeper, he thinks: "Could it be some allusion? Could the Marshal be so discreet as to have come across some clues and yet not wish to say more? Or is he playing with me? He has caught me in his trap and he is playing with me."

With these thoughts clouding over him, at a certain moment Sanatescu looks towards the door that leads into the anteroom, after which he switches his eyes to the other door opening into a small suite. He thinks: "What if Antonescu got wind about our doings and is now playing with me like a cat plays with a mouser while all along he has men waiting behind the doors to arrest me?!" But he knows that when Antonescu grows angry he sweats profusely and he reflexively lifts his hand to his pocket. He is waiting for that gesture to occur.

Most embarrassing that such feelings should exist between two men who have been life-long friends! And yet it is this very life which at a given time compels one to forget the great dreams and pleasant adventures and even the very years spent together in youth. Without making you become actual enemies, life does nevertheless make you feel that you belong elsewhere, that you are prompted by other interests. Interests of such moment that one forgets about friendship and about likes and dislikes and about everything, and one points the gun at the person who sentimentally one feels the propensity to be fond of. The general drawls, as if he not convinced of his own words: "That was some time ago... Nowadays Ica comes only sporadically; he has not time enough to tutor the king..." He gazes at the Marshal with a simulated nonchalance and gives a start when the latter says menacingly: "Yes, indeed, only sporadically!..."

Wrought up, General Sanatescu observes each small gesture, each small movement the Marshal makes. He tries to set his mind at rest by thinking that most likely it is an exaggeration of his own imagination. He must be composed, keep calm and not let himself be carried away by feelings. That's the way life is! Youth is generous, romantic, exuberant, while maturity requires reason. History is full of incidents about brothers who played together in their infancy and killed one another for power when they grew up!

He broods over these ideas but not in order to take courage. Because here it is not a matter of taking courage. Here it is a matter of aridity, cynicism, world-wearing which as one advances in age, earthly interests impose upon one. Interests which by virtue of reason dehumanize one, bring one to such states as the present one when they, two men of about sixty years of age, are, should their interest require it, capable of carrying out grave deeds against each other.

Sanatescu is sad. He is experiencing an embarrassing feeling of compromise and barrenness, of slavery to certain forces outside himself, forces which are abstractly and rigidly called "'higher reasons" and which mean in fact the alienation of man from his normal feelings. How he would like to be young and exuberant once again, and take the man facing him by the arm, a man who would no longer be withered and red with malevolence and hardened by vanity and interests, and to relish with him the pleasures of champagne parties given by elegant cavalry lieutenants in the company of merry ballet girls from the musical-comedy theatre.

But everything is an illusion. Now they are aged sour tempered men urged by interests which could induce them to kill each other with cynicism. He adopts a soft voice, which is not his usual one, and says: "Ion, that's the very reason I came over here for; your visits to the Palace have indeed become too sporadic... " He stares straight into the expressionless steel-like eyes, eyes which were once blue, and very well aware of the purpose of the invitation, aware that Antonescu might not leave the palace alive, he does nonetheless convey it to him: "You should, I think, resume your habit of dining at the palace from time to time. Take it as you will, but I have come to invite you officially to the palace. Well, let's say Saturday, yes, Saturday would be a very good day..."

Antonescu does not let such an opportunity slip by: "Why ; should I come?! To have a closer look at the people plotting against me?!... Do you think I have any pleasure in meeting that haughty Greek woman and that snuffing son of hers?!..." He is fuming. When he, remembers about "the Palace" he works himself up into a state of fury. Because, in his dictator's psychology, he feels like taking revenge on all that does not submit to him or all that he cannot subject. It is in vain that Sanatescu says: "Besides all these aspects, Ion, there is the country, the interests of the nation!" Malevolence seizes Antonescu's body like a vaccine. Monomania blocks his mind and he no longer takes into account that he is in the presence of an old friend who reminds him that he too is a man, that he too experienced an exuberant youth made up of daily pleasures. He proclaims as if from the height of a pedestal: "I am the nation!... Nobody knows the interests of the nation better than I do!..." And he apostrophizes Sanatescu: "Matache, you aren't somehow... Well, I never!" He is no longer the friend, now he is the dictator: "You are very well aware that I sent you to the Palace as a loyal representative of mine. And you are also well aware that I entrusted you with the mission of counteracting all that is rotten in the institution of the Palace!"

Sanatescu knows him only too well and he also knows that he flies into this state of sufficiency most rapidly. And most particularly he knows that he feels most at ease when he is in the grasp of such a state. He answers in a dry, polite tone of voice: "I quite understand, sir, Marshal..." But this attitude is not good either, for Antonescu cuts him short with: "Don't talk to me like that!..." He has scarcely succeeded in holding himself back from shouting, but he blurts out: "Don't you speak to me like that! I am your closest friend; you haven't got a better and an older friend than myself; you haven't the right not to believe in me!"

The general's even temper lends him the superiority of patient politeness. The disdainful look of surprise on his face gives way to an expression of urgency: "If you want me to believe in you, you must give me proof of your lucidity. You may send me before the firing squad, but I tell you all this because we have spent a lifetime together. I came here because I was convinced you were aware of everything: we are witnessing a decisive week!... It is the last one when you still have time to take a decision. You must break away from the Germans, Ion, otherwise... "

And while Antonescu threateningly asks him what he means by "otherwise", he shakes his head with sadness and makes the gesture of disaster, of the final, total disaster.

The idea of disaster does not impress the Marshal in the least. On the contrary, it offers him the opportunity of displaying his superiority. He lifts from the table the text of the cable dispatched to General Wilson and hands it to Sanatescu: "I have given thought to these matters too," he says cooling down at the thought of the superiority he was demonstrating, "I have asked General Wilson to help me obtain more advantageous conditions for a truce. And even more than that, Matache, just before you came, I told Dr. Clodius to inform Hitler that I want to withdraw from the war and therefore I urgently request the assent of Germany!"... He is satisfied with himself and so he remembers his friendship with the general: "You see, we think alike!" he says attempting to appease him for having previously lost control of his temper. Sanatescu, however, does not respond to his attempt at warmth. He is anxious.

He had, for a moment, hoped that all was right with Antonescu. He had come to think that reason and lucidity dominated Antonescu's mind and he had sincerely hoped that there would be no need of subterfuges between them. He had even come to be glad that life did not oblige him to participate in the radical measures against his old friend. That things were taking such a course that, by refuting the fear he felt in connection with Antonescu's dictatorial propensity, they assist him in not having to point his gun at the man alongside whom he had spent such a beautiful youth... But this idea of asking the Germans, of asking paranoiac Hitler to give his assent instantly aggrieved him so much that he paid no attention to the details and did not therefore notice Antonescu's change of attitude. Alerted, he asks him: "Do you really expect to get Hitler's assent, Ion, do you really?"

Antonescu confirms with majestic pride. He seems to be most proud of and delighted with his idea, a fact which alerts the general even more: "Ion, don't do such a foolish thing! Hitler may seize you, dominate you as he did Horthy, and occupy the country with his troops!... "

Self-assured, Antonescu answers: "I don't think so. I have weighed things thoroughly. At such moments, when the population is agitated and some are attempting to rise in rebellion, I need Hitler. His armies bring balance to the country, they do!... And by this gesture of mine I am teaching him a lesson of what honesty means. And, you must know, my lessons have quite an impact on Hitler! ... Chivalry obliges me to give him notice. We are soldiers and men of character, Matache. A person with a sense of decency about him cannot but appreciate our gesture! Hitler will appreciate it, and..."

He is content. Content and confident of his gesture, his power of thought and reason. He is so confident and satisfied that he overlooks the growing anxiety with which Sanatescu is listening to him. Sanatescu knows that his megalomania makes him become extremely incited even about his political errors. Now they, two elderly generals, are standing before the map of the front. Antonescu points to yesterday's and this morning's alignments drawing the following conclusion: "The situation on the front is not unusually difficult. Whenever an army launches an offensive, it does it forcibly. The secret consists in giving ground scientifically, letting the enemy grind his energy to no avail. Therefore, and I'm saying it as a fact not just to take heart, the Russian offensive doesn't scare me too much. It is painful only because they are making headway on our territory; and that is an entirely different matter, but if we examine things carefully, we will find that they, in this very war, were pushed at one assault tenfold farther back than we have been in these last two days. I have here the latest communiques received this evening"... he says taking hold of a dossier labeled top-secret. "Here, the Germans declare that, ... by rallying the troops from large areas and by bringing in fresh forces, the highly threatened sectors of the front have been reinforced. That means that Hitler has come to recognize the realism of my requests and has ordered that the divisions of armored cars should be sent to our assistance. Now they must be on their way. You see, Matache, by asking permission to withdraw from the war, I gave at the same time an ultimatum claiming the grouping of forces on the Romanian battlefront. With a powerful German army of armored cars, coupled with our forces, I can hold the Focsani-Namoloasa-Galatzi front in the face of the Russians for at least six months. That is why, concurrently with the rallying of our army in the most powerful zone of our country and owing to the bold resistance put up by Friessner's armies and the reinforcements coming to his assistance, the Russian offensive will abate. This very morning I noticed that it has begun to flag and that its moment of great impetus has passed. Here are two Orders of the Day of the Supreme Soviet Staff Headquarters dated today, 22 August, which we received and decoded this evening. The first one is addressed to Marshall Malinovsky and it draws his attention to the danger posed by, look here, the powerful defensive enemy line which is echeloned in the North-West part of Jassy..' And here is the second one cabled to Army General Tolbukhin warning him that the enemy defensive line is highly reinforced and disposed in depth to the South of Tighina... All this is obvious enough, isn't it? I am speaking to you as you see, with arguments acknowledged by the enemy. And, - he added with satisfaction while lifting a slip of paper from the table - here is what the neutral newspapers say this evening! It is a translation from the Swedish newspaper 'Afton Tidningen' code-transmitted by our Legation there: ... the fighting on the Third Ukrainian Front is becoming more and more violent due to the increase of German resistance: Soviet war correspondents report that the Germans have succeeded in breaking through certain parts of the Russian lines... This is the situation, my dear Matache, which entitles me to say - and over the twenty-five years that I have been on the General Staff I have never one erred - that I, with my army and the German reinforcements can hold out for at least six months along the - fortified front. And the Focsani -Namoloasa-Galatzi line is my work, the outcome of my strategic thinking for which, as you well know, others were praised during World War I. But that is net of any importance! What is important is that it gave the expected results and that the Germans were defeated because of it. Now, over the four years of the war, I have managed to make of it a major fortified zone in Europe. I did it with this very end in view, namely, that the Russians might reach this far! But, mark my words, I say neither that I will defeat them, nor that I will push them back. I say only, after a mature deliberation, that I can hold them back for a minimum of six months. And in six months the tide of the war can be reversed and to what measure. .. The Anglo-Americans will have time to think things over. Hitler will have time to perfect his secret weapons. Yes, I have seen them being experimented. I am convinced that, the latest next spring, that is in early 1945, the world will witness the terrifying power of the new weapons!..."

He is not only convinced himself, but his arguments are able to convict his friend: "I shall hold the Russians back. And then the Russians are not interested in descending towards Bucharest. Their route now leads upwards, towards Czechoslovakia, Austria and Berlin. They will maintain the occupied zone in Moldavia to be able ultimately to cross directly into Transylvania, Poland, and Hungary and finally reach the German frontier. And I, by ensuring them a peaceful passage by the route leading across the Eastern Carpathians, will obtain any armistice conditions I want. That is what I have reasoned and I am sure!... Logical and pragmatically sure!... What do you say to it?"... And then he added with the tone of a man who has pondered over these matters for a long time: "My rezoning and conditions of a strategist tell me that I can hold back the destiny of the war for at least six months and that it is only in this way that I can rid the country of disturbing unrest."

General Sanatescu does not need much time to give an answer. He has known Antonescu's strategic reasoning since they were in military school together, forty years ago. That is why he asks without any hesitation: "Well, yes, everything is quite clear but did you ever think about the fact that under such conditions the war would destroy the country more and more?"

Antonescu remains calm; yes, he has given thought to that matter, of course he has! He has thought out and has calculated accurately all he says: "The country must help me, it must make every sacrifice to help me eventually get out of the fix!"

Yes, indeed, this is Antonescu, the Antonescu he has no longer anything in common with. These are his limits. Sanatescu clearly realizes now that the danger resides in Anonescu's high strategic thinking, in his very mentality: the strategist is perfect, but the sacrifices of the country are too calculated and decided; to a certain extent it is he who has to get out of the mess as best he can! ... Sanatescu tries, nonetheless, to caution him with regard to the most serious aspect of the matter: "Therefore, Moldavia will be occupied and the war will be waged on its territory; that means everything turned to ashes. The Russians will strike across the mountains, through Transylvania where the Germans and Hungarians will put up a strong defense fighting for each inch of land; that means again turning everything into ashes and ruin.

And you will remain with a third of the country under your control. A third of the country that will be bombed and drained of all its energy and rendered unable to support an army!..."

Hearing the calamitous ring of his own words, or better said the ghastly meaning of the words uttered by him, Sanatescu stops short. But Antonescu has remained unimpressed: "Exactly so," he retorts boldly being so confident, that Sanatescu barely utters: "Well, yes, but what about the country?!..." To which question he receives the unflinchingly convinced response: "The country? It is not the self-moment in the history when we shall take refuge in the mountains if needs be!... But, after it, the country will flourish and prosper. The occidentals will arrive here and we will not confront more with the Red Danger!..."

Heaving reason, total geostrategic reason, proud of his visionary way of thinking, he has begun to speak grandiloquently. His highly lucid and careful reasoning has roused unexpected powers in him. Once again he turns from the skilled strategist into the dictator who is convinced that he is the only man who can aggrandize the country.

Sanatescu's countenance is empty of any expression. He is silent and empty like a court-of-justice hall after the sentence has been passed. He feels lonely in this office. He feels lonelier perhaps than he has ever felt before. He gazes at his former friend as if he were an inanimate object: something maid of iron or cement, or stone. All is clear-cut an measured, there is no chance of changing anything; he can't obtain any compromise from his friend, to gain a possibility to save him by the cynical reasons of the others. He felt the need to forget this friendly intention and to be not sentimental. Since his reasoning had made him approach and join the men who were organizing Antonescu's overthrow, he had had a feeling of goliath. Rationally, he was working shoulder to shoulder with the people of the National Democratic Bloc; but sentimentally, he felt the need to have it out with Antonescu.

But now he knows he can never have it out with Antonescu. Things are so serious that only reason must be taken into account. And reason has shown him that Antonescu has sufficient arguments to stick to his guns. He is sound-minded enough to know what he is after and what he can attain. And this makes him the more dangerous, demonstrating that he must inexorably be removed. For the very reason that what he says is possible, for the very raison that he would be able to delay the progress of the war for minimum six months. But at what a cost!... Good, God, at what a cost!?... And another reason: Will they found, after six months the same possibility to escape by Hitler?!... If the Soviets, as they have done not once, will change them politics?! If they provokes and begin a global working class conflict against the Westerners using Hitler, with his last forces but new weapons, like an ally?! Even Antonescu calculated in his strategy this Hitler's necessary time to put into the service his weapons!... Certainly: the today's timeliness to turn weapons, will be missed; the Romania's train is missing!

Henceforth, Sanatescu starts to control his every gesture and word. He has taken a decision and he is most careful lest he might rouse the Marshal's suspicions.

This hour of night elapses in a cold, hectic atmosphere, as if a guillotine had been dropped at some moment or other. The general straightens his back as if filling in the shape of his smartly tailored blue suit and seeks to speak in a conventional tone: "Well, you haven't answered my question: are you going to accept the invitation to have lunch with His Majesty?..."

Sensing the formal shift that the discussion has acquired, Antonescu answers coldly: "No, I can't. Inform the king that in the New House it is too hot, it's stifling and it harms my aorta. I can't waste two hours to get an egg and an apple, for that's what I have for lunch. I have acquainted you with the situation at the front and the reckonings I have made. Report them to the royal family and let them bear them well in mind" - he added while Sanatescu asked the question: "And can you not come on Wednesday, Thursday, Friday or Saturday, do you mean to say you aren't going to pay a visit to the Palace before you leave for the front?"

Antonescu reflects for a while. Or maybe, reluctant to do something against his wish, he delays in giving an answer: "As you said too, I think Saturday would be best - he replies with disgust - at about 10 o'clock in the morning. Because at 1 o'clock I want to offer lunch to the cabinet and to the German mission, to announce them of my intention to move permanently to the front. But I shall come to see the king before that, don't worry, I shall come!"

Sanatescu is not worrying. Concomitantly with the Marshal's words - "Saturday"... "at about 10 o'clock"... "because at 1 o'clock" ... therefore concomitantly with these words he rehearsed in his mind the plan for arresting the Marshal drawn up by the conspirators: "Saturday, 26 August, at about noon, when the Germans are having lunch"... Now a new detail had appeared - the luncheon offered by Antonescu to the government and the German mission. Well, they would have the chance to arrest them all at one go. And while still contemplating the variants to the plan of arresting them, he says to the Marshal on his departure: "If you don't come on Saturday, we will go to the front with you!"...

They shake hands and he leaves. On reaching the anteroom, Sanatescu glances again at the doors behind which he expected there were men waiting to arrest him. He passes by the aides with a look of dignity on his face and when, entering his car, he reacquires the feeling of security and begins to feel pity for Antonescu: it had not occurred to Antonescu; but as for himself, he couldn't afford not to have him arrested. Behind his doors indeed there will be... The engine of his car droning smoothly, the general surveys the details of the plan for arresting Antonescu and his government. This very evening during the secret meeting due to be held on Columbus street he will have to warn the involved persons about the 1 o'clock lunch where both the members of the cabinet and of the German military mission may be placed under arrest. Having been invited by the Marshal, they will all come without the slightest shade of suspicion.

Making these calculations the last traces of sentimentalism vanish, thus setting his mind free: "Life is, after all, harsh. It is even cruel to us. It has so many reasons which we have grown accustomed to calling 'higher' that it leaves only very little room for our sincere and spontaneous experiences."

His car enters by the palace gate, it runs along the alleys of the park and it pulls up in front of the New House. In his faultlessly tailored dark-blue suit which he almost always wears when he goes to conspiratorial meetings, tall, distinguished and self-important, General Sanatescu heads for the king's office. He salutes and announces everybody with a loud voice that Antonescu refuses to come to lunch. Then, drawing the king aside, he tells him in the same breath: "We must have him arrested, no doubt. And that as fast as possible. It is extremely dangerous to give time for the Hitler's weapons. The Marshal has a strategic plan which is unfortunately sound and highly to his advantage. He knows that at the cost of dividing the country, he can hold back the Russian advance for at least six months. And he is determined to carry out his plan in order to obtain the most advantageous conditions of armistice possible. He explained it to me on the map. It is a well-planned strategy which he will put into effect to the letter. We must have him arrested without delay; before he carries his plan through. He said he would come on Saturday at 10 o'clock in the morning, but... I tell you with all my military skill, it is a well-grounded strategic plan."

The king remains meditative for some time, then he says: "All right, I have just sent after Lucretiu Patrascanu. He told me he would lie low till 26 August, so I have called him over for a last interview. If the situation is so grave, we shall necessarily have to find out exactly how with stand with the military preparations. I should ask Patrascanu if he is sure on some workers movement promised by that engineer Ceausu. He did not specify to Damaceanu how many civilians may sustain the army."

Sanatescu answers promptly, like a skilled officer who has made a battle plan in his mind: "As to the military preparations I arranged with Damaceanu for all the Bucharest's troops. He is confident in that communist commando; but a commando is no more than a commando! We need units and strategy against a more then possible counter-attack"...

....

The preparation by the Patrascanu's collaborators of a printing house for a special newspaper issue which should mobilize the entire country. The situation of the clandestine preparations within the army; the setting up of the military units located around Bucharest. As a precautionary measure, the King's Proclamation to the nation is recorded in advance, so that it may be broadcast at the established time even if he happened to be immobilized by any incident. Lucretiu Patrascanu draws up the first two major state decrees to be proclaimed by the new government for the fast democratization of the country and the release of all political prisoners, so as to be launched right after the proclamation of the new government and to be published in the mentioned special newspaper issue.

LVI

The disciplined, prompt and impervious Eugen Cristescu is invariably of late the last to enter the Marshal's office at the end of the working day. He appears at the word of command like a well-oiled mechanism which starts off noiselessly at the right moment and works meticulously, thus doubtlessly proving its utility.

He gives his reports promptly, in a clear military jargon, behind the wording of which a refined ability of deduction and a keen insight into matters can be sensed. These qualities enable him to be totally unostentatious and to conceal to perfection his foxlike cunning of a policeman. Sometimes, when he thinks more profoundly about it, ant when he is sincere with himself, Antonescu is obliged to admit that this is the only man he would truly be afraid of. Because he plays his role of correctness to such perfection that it is a certain fact he would be capable of extremely incorrect acts, and that without ever rousing the slightest hint of a suspicion.

In 1940, when Antonescu came to power, he removed Eugen Bianu from the function of chief of the State Security Forces as he considered him to be faithful to Carol II. Apart from him, he fired several other co-workers.

Like any true professional who knows the rules of the game, Cristescu who was one of the persons dismissed, withdrew without making any fuss and became a strictly private citizen. He broke off relations with everybody thus giving absolutely no opportunity to be caught in the wrong by the agents assigned to shadow him by the man who had taken over his place and job. Like in a typical English thriller he became a passionate flower cultivator and a passionate fisherman appearing to have forgotten everything about his previous occupation.

In spite of this, during the iron-guards rebellion when Antonescu ordered the army to take measures against the extremist guards, when the entire State Security Force and police were looking for the iron-guards chiefs and could not find them anywhere, Ion Antonescu received a phone-call. At the other end of the line spoke Eugen Cristescu, the peaceful flower cultivator, passionate fisherman and distinguished concert-goer who, according to the very accurate information handed in by his shadows who unflinchingly kept close watch on his every movement had wholly given up everything that could have even reminded one of his past dealings and profession. Without the slightest trace of ostentation, in a genuinely modest voice and putting it in a very matter-of-fact manner, he told Antonescu the following: "Excuse my disturbing you, sir; but I ask your permission to take only two minutes of your most precious time. It has accidentally come within my hearing that the police and the State Security Forces are assiduously looking for the former Deputy Premier and ring-leader of the rebels, Mr Horia Sima. If somehow the information I am in possession of is correct and the State Security Forces and the police have indeed not yet managed to find him over the last three days, and I beg my pardon if I am mistaken, please allowed me to inform you upon the fact that, yesterday, Mr. Horia Sima was seen in the Ioanid house, at the corner between the Polona and Dacia streets, and he left last night at about 8.20 p.m. for Bragadiru commune. This morning he was seen there climbing into a grey car belonging to the German Wehrmacht, the license number of which

I regret I am unable to give you now. Riding in this car he arrived at Giuirgiu at about 9.31. At Giurgiu he hid in the boot of the same grey car and crossed our frontier into Bulgaria only twenty minutes ago. At present he is in the building of the German Commander at Ruse. With all my respects, I once again apologize for having taken the liberty of disturbing you, sir. And I thank you most warmly for your kindness of having answered my phone call."

The very next day, by high order, the special Intelligence Service pertaining to the Ministry of Home Affairs became directly attached to the Premier's office and Eugen Cristescu was appointed its chief. A function which he has held since then always irreproachably correct in carrying out the Marshal's orders. So very correct that the latter has never dared to ask him about his connections with the British and American Intelligence Services. He has become his right-hand man in efficiently solving the most ticklish problems and over the last period of time together with Piki Vasiliu, the Undersecretary of State in the Ministry of Home Affairs, he has been called upon by the Marshal to form together with him a council of three, to decide and discuss upon the most delicate and top secret issues which never pass through the Council of Ministers and to which even the Minister of Home Affairs, General D. Popescu-Codita, has no access.

General D. Popescu-Codita, once appointed as their superior, has not been discharged from his post by Antonescu only due to inertia and to the fact that he does not want to publicly admit certain weaknesses by reshuffling the government; yet, now and again, the rumor is spread that the Marshal wants to send him to a provincial garrison. The Minister of Home° Affairs, this General Popescu, whose name is never pronounced without the funny nickname attached to it (Codita is the Romanian for "short little tail"), is somewhat of a social climber and an upstart. He is arrogant and conceited, and this irritates the Marshal, the more so as he behaves slavishly and humbly towards himself. He made a bad choice, which now he corrects only de facto, but leaves as it is from the de jure point of view,: in order not to compromise the prestige of his leadership by replacing the very Minister of Home Affairs. Yet Dumitru Popescu-Codita disgusts him. It is said that as a general, he imposes himself mostly by his self-sufficiency, by putting on airs and by appointing nincompoops whom he can dominate, men who belong to the mental category of obtuse, stupid and vicious first-sergeants who are faithful servants to him. The social surroundings in the midst of which he has spent a good part of his life, the military milieu, does not take him very much in earnest in spite of the peacock airs he puts on, a milieu within which he is much more frequently called by his nickname than by his actual name. Quite often, instead of being called General Popescu he is merely called Popescu-Codita. He is aware of it, and, evidently, feels the Marshal's disdain and also senses how little he is trusted in the government and that, whenever there is an important decision to be taken, he is replaced by his two subordinates. But he keeps it pent up within himself, happy and thankful not to be replaced and sent to the battlefront.

Hence, the presence of Cristescu, discreet and conscientious as usual, is welcome, he giving the marshal in his silent, highly professional way of discharging his duties, more certainty than the whale Ministry of the Home Affairs does. Without any emphasis, he tersely reports the secret events of the day: the Minister of Communications, Atta Constantinescu, whose father used to be styled Constantinescu-the-Swine in the political spheres of the pre-war period, has informed the king that the civilian ministers in the government - Busila, Marinescu, Petrovici, Tomescu and himself are ready to hand in their resignations. Thus, by expressing their disagreement with Antonescu's policy, they are endeavoring to bring about a government crisis. All this, of course, is being prompted by their political leaders, Mr Maniu and Mr Bratianu.

Angry about this piece of news, the Marshal exclaims disdainfully: "Let them take over the Premiership; I offered it to them before! Did you take my message to Maniu?"

It is only the rational coolness of the professional spy that tranquillizes him: "Sir, forty-five minutes ago Mr Maniu left the palace where Mr Mihalache joined him only five minutes after he had left your office. I considered it inadequate to tackle him immediately. He could have suspected that he had been followed. I left word at his place and I'm expecting his answer to arrive any time... I know, I know exactly what you are going to say: we might receive his answer in two months from now. Please, sir, rest assured: he will receive me this very evening, that is if he does not pretext he wants to sleep; and if he does, you may rely on my bringing you the answer at seven-thirty tomorrow morning."

His precision assuages the Marshal. After the departure of the chief of his Intelligence Service, he orders a list comprising the military Undersecretaries of the ministries directed by civilians to be drawn up for him. He will appoint then provisional ministers the very moment the ministers hand in their resignations, thus preventing the possibility of a government crisis.

Having taken this measure, he meditates on how useful Cristescu is to him. For Cristescu, with his refined method of disclosing information gradually, told him just before leaving that details regarding his latest visit to Hitler had been divulged at the Palace about a week ago. Mihai Antonescu had been suspect number one as the other persons who had accompanied him were respectable experienced officers who knew only too well the meaning of a secret in time of war. But the suspicion had proved to be wrong. The information had been revealed by Eugen Bianu, the former General director of the State Security Forces who had preserved the function of Vice-Chairman of the International Organization of State Security. He in his turn had been informed by an Allied agency which, most probably, had its informers among Hitler's camarilla at Rastenburg.

....

LVIII

After descending the stairs of the Premiership building, the Marshal climbs into his car, but not before giving his aide, who is accompanying him the order that for tomorrow's Council of Ministers only the military ministers should be convened so that any possible resignation of the civilian ministers should be avoided. Then his car starts, heading for Antonescu's home at Snagov.

On the way, he notices that the car is being driven not by his personal driver, Major Caloenescu, but by a captain. He inquires into the matter and Major Georgescu, the commanding officer of his personal guard, explains to him that he is away on some urgent call. The Marshal makes no comment and does not suspect anything. He is much too tired for that.

....

Now, your telegram sent to the Allies!... What a fantastic day! Quite fantastic!... Yes, there is something up, yes..."

III. THE TWENTY-THIRD OF AUGUST

....

II

The king is sitting at his desk with the latest map of the front spread out in front of him. He is extremely excited. Patrascanu has just given him in a diplomatic manner neither good nor bad information concerning the engineer Ceausu and his commando which will act, but insisted on the idea of the anti-Hitler of the population trying to assume it as a merit of the communists. Patrascanu and Grigore Niculescu-Buzesti, slightly leaning forward towards the king, are sitting in the two armchairs on the opposite side of the desk; Mircea Ioanitiu is trying to catch a foreign post on the radio while Mocioni-Stircea, more nervous and impulsive by nature, is pacing the room to and fro, under the pretext of checking whether there is any suspect movement on the corridor.

Niculescu-Buzesti has taken the initiative of conducting matters this time. This can be felt by the way he opens the discussion and by the place he occupies, sitting by the king and Patrascanu. He seems to have been entrusted with a special mission and Patrascanu does not like that. He even makes the remark: "Mr Buzesti, I can't help feeling that you intend to take Mr Maniu's place at this meeting: he being absent, we seem to feel the painful need of having somebody who should attend to things being postponed and delayed, and here you are, offering yourself to perform this duty!... I personally agree what Sanatescu told to His Majesty. Beginning with this very moment, the insurrection can start any time. We are no longer in a position to admit of any delays, however desirous you may be to play Mr Maniu's part..."

The king and the other two politicians smile discreetly, recalling the stately attitude Maniu adopted when withdrawing from the room only an hour before. But they make no comment. They have established that this evening they should meet the representatives of the parties in turn in order to arrive at certain agreements with each one in part. Buzesti, sensing Patrascanu's tenseness, seeks to present things in a more favorable angle in order to gain his favor: "As a matter of fact, we too must inform you that Mr Maniu, here, in the presence of His Majesty, accepted the formula of the cabinet and he is ready to proceed to making it up; at the same time has made a concession to you..." He pauses to see the effect of his words on his interlocutor's red face and then he specifies: "Mr Maniu consents to your taking over the Ministry of Justice, provided you accept to take it temporarily..:" Than he explains: "That is you will take it over for the several days required to pass all the decrees; then you will be replaced by a specialist as we must observe the principle we agreed upon with regard to the government being formed of specialists, in which the representatives of the parties were to enter but without a portfolio".

Patrascanu has already made up-his mind. His quick brain has already thought out everything, it has made its choice and it has drawn its conclusions in a way which will enable him to take the offensive, So, the instant Niculescu-Buzesti finishes his sentence, he replies on the spot: "With a view to the crucial issues lying ahead of us, I have no intention of further commenting on your reserved attitude; I accept. Your Majesty, if the formation of the government depends on my consent, then you have my agreement loyally expressed here and I request our proceeding with urgency to the forming of the entire government."

Niculescu-Buzesti does not have to employ his highly intuitive mental qualities to understand that he has been surpassed completely by Patrascanu. It is quite obviously so and an expression of pleased surprise appears on the king's face. The diplomat says that, after all, a meeting of the representatives of the parties making up the National Democratic Bloc has been established for the next day. This remark serves Patrascanu's purpose and he answers promptly: "We don't have to wait till tomorrow. If we decide all today, our agitation is finishing and we can wait discreetly for the Saturday. For this reason is not necessary to risk more a meeting; you can let Mr Maniu know tonight that I have agreed if, of course, my consenting or not is the only hindrance to proceeding further; I am not interested in becoming your Excellency; all I want is to be certain that I can pass the democratization's decrees and to see this government arrested"...

But tonight is the night of Niculescu-Buzesti's eruption of - personality. He who is at the same time Mihai Antonescu's, Maniu's and the king's man, certainly feels the favorable moment has arrived for the crowning of his career and he dares give advice openly: "As a matter of fact, from this point of view, I think it is quite indifferent as to what exactly happens for, to my mind, the Constitutional Factor, meaning by this Your Majesty, should replace, not arrest the government ! Forgive me, but the king is the supreme authority, the king cannot act like any ordinary conspirator."

This is enough to make even the king lose his temper. He rivets his eyes on the ambitious diplomat and states: "Victor Immanuel and Mussolini had exactly the same type of conflict. And in spite of everything you or others may say, the king of Italy plotted against the dictator and had him arrested. By fighting arm in hand against Hitler's ally, the House of Savoy did not compromise its name, quite on the contrary, it gained the country's confidence."

The discussion has flared up. Only Patrascanu is satisfied and smiles encouragingly to the king. He is glad to see his own point of view embraced by this young man who is quite inexperienced but who has been forced by necessity to choose his fate in one way or another and who has opted for the radical solution. Polite, Niculescu-Buzesti, guessing Patrascanu's approval of the king's attitude, attempts to expound Mr Maniu's theory according to which Antonescu should sign the armistice and command the turning of arms against Hitler. But the king is adamant: "General Mihail is faithful to the Throne and he will therefore direct the combat against the Germans much better because he hates them from the bottom of his heart!... I want you to know I will not make any compromises. If we stick to this categorical course, we shall have the approbation of all the population in the country and we shall have only the German troops standing against us. The question is how we can annihilate or to prevent them reaction; so..."

The atmosphere has cleared up and becomes more intimate Buzesti, being a commonsensical man, has nothing else to add but that he will have Leucutia remind Maniu, every other hour, about drawing up the list of the members of the cabinet. And as they have been smoking very much, the king, Ioanitiu and Stircea being chain smokers, they leave the king's office, cross the wide corridor and go into the yellow drawing-room where the air is fresh and hot coffee is waiting for them. Coming directly from the military conference which took place in Columbus Street, General Sanatescu and General Vasiliu-Rascanu enter through the open door of the neighboring dining-room. The latter acquaints them with the fact that he has cancelled the departure for the front of the Slatina Division and that he has arranged with the General Staff Headquarters for it to be sent over to Bucharest. The General Staff studies other similar possibilities.

At two-thirty everything is clarified, the decisions are taken with great accuracy and, confirming as "H hour" the midday of the 26 of August, the telegram addressed to the Allies is drafted. Ion Mocioni-Stircea follows to go personally to have it transmitted by the special Code Service of the Ministry of Foreign Affairs which receives the respective order of Niculescu-Buzesti.

Patrascanu is satisfied with the outcome. Now he can take leave from everybody present till 26 August in the afternoon that is till the hour when the insurrection is to be launched.

....

At Snagov, in a palace in the proximity of Bucharest used as a place of refuge, Marshal Antonescu makes ready for his meeting with Clodius in an attempt to make him pay all the debts owed by Germany to Romania. A review of the brutal attempts by Germany to take control over the Romanian economy.

Meanwhile, secret negotiations go on between the Soviets and the Romanian Marshal to establish the terms of an armistice acceptable to both sides, negotiations carried on in Stockholm between the Soviet ambassadress Alexandra Kollontay and the

Romanian ambassador Fr. Nanu. Sometime ago, this one informed the Marshal that: "...the Russian counselor Semenov handed me a note transmitted by the Soviets to the government Antonescu <avec lequel nous preferons avoir a faire>, containing the Kremlin's claim to this government to part from the Germans making union with the Soviets... After it, even the ambassadress Kollontay convoked the plenipotentiary Romanian minister Nanu repeating him the same mentioned proposal"...

The negotiations had continued with the mentioned Marshal's efforts to obtain the most acceptable terms of an armistice. Now, he has a clear diplomatic signal of success and waits every hour for the revised Soviet claims, to answer about his accept and to go on the battlefront to sign the armistice.

Description of the Antonescu's hopes in this respect, while waiting for the telegram with the terms of the armistice which singles him out to negotiate with the Soviets.

VII

The sun rises later, at twenty-eight minutes past five. The blazing explosion of its light collides with the windscreen of the car driven at top speed by Ion Mocioni-Stircea. Master of Hunting of the Palace, it is the most cynical character of the king's camarilla, more aged then the others and involved in all kind of secret adventures.

It appears emerging from the crowns of the trees, blinding him, and then it disappears projecting the shadows of the tall, slender poplars growing at the side of the highroad, on to the windscreen of his car.

It is the Bucharest-Ploiesti highroad. The Baron is racing, at break-neck speed and is fully relishing it. He turns the car abruptly to the right along the road leading to Snagov, enjoying the screeching of the tires as the car goes round the band. After driving for another few minutes up the road, he hides the car in the forest and thin walks along a side pathway leading to the villa where the Code-Service is concealed. He is greeted by Radulescu-Pogoneanu who, announced by Buzesti, is waiting for him in the doorway with the non-committal play of feature of a man who has to code and decode messages, transmit them and then forget them. But even he, when he reads what he is to cable, becomes excited and looks at Stircea in a manner which betrays the degree of his excitement. For, indeed, he is holding in his hands, hands which have operated many a secret message, perhaps the most important of all.

Signed by Iuliu Maniu, Dinu Bratianu, Constantin-Titel Petrescu and Lucretiu Patrascanu, on behalf of the four parties composing the National Democratic Bloc, the telegram communicates to the Allies that in Romania it has been decided that the action to overthrow the pro-Hitler regime of Ion Antonescu will take place on 26 August at noon through the starting of an armed insurrection. The Allied armies are required to afford assistance to the launching of the insurrection by promptly making certain air attacks. The Military Committee of the Insurrection establishes how the assistance should be given in order to support the unleashing at noon of the insurrection by the Allied air force simultaneously bombing the five objectives listed numerically: (1) the German military camp at Baneasa; (2) the Baneasa and Zimnicea aerodromes; (3) the German aerodromes and air force units at Apahida, Szolnok, Seghedin and Belgrade; (4) the bridges over the Theiss at Szolnok and over the Danube at Belgrade; (5) two railway junctions in Hungary, in order to render impossible the transportation of the Hungarian army which has been massed at the frontier with Romania. The sixth point indicates that the two American and British commando brigades should land at Popesti-Leordeni aerodrome.

Excited, Pogoneanu gets down to coding the cable in order to transmit it with all haste. He tells Baron Mocioni-Stircea that if he wishes to witness the dispatch of the message he may wait for twenty to thirty minutes - the time required for him to code its. In the meantime he may go either into one of the bedrooms of the villa to have a rest or into the park on the shore of the lake,

Baron Mocioni-Stircea chooses neither the bedroom, nor the park; he prefers a dip in the take which he hopes will refresh him after his sleepless night. The lake is crystal-clear and, cool ant the sun-light reflected on its surface glazes it with a mercury-red color. Casting off his clothes, the baron sportingly plunges into the lake and swims swiftly taking delight in advancing towards the sun-rise through the soothing smooth water.

But, suddenly, his solitary sporting pleasure is disturbed. At this early morning hour when he is free of all burdens and is swimming among the water-lilies, a great shadow is cast across his realm of peace and leisure.

It is a boat. A boat rowed by a man dressed in an immaculate military tunic. The baron not only recognizes him as being Colonel Radu Davidescu, the Marshal's principal military secretary, but also realizes that he has given himself away. He experiences a moment of embarrassment. Fortunately the water hides his nakedness and obliges him to keep exerting his arms in order to keep afloat, thus enabling him not to betray his panic through gestures. He swims another stroke and makes up his mind: he raises his head out of the water and greets the colonel with so familiar a smile that the latter, astounded, admits the game as such as if they had met there in the deep water in front of the palace every day at this early hour. Without constraint, the baron gets into the light boat which is being rowed by the colonel whose sartorial correctness proves insufficient to conceal his perplexity. The baron smiles at the colonel in the attitude of a gambler playing cards and he says: "You have caught me swimming in the Marshal's territorial waters; but you must understand I entered them without any intention whatever!"

The colonel is stunned: sitting here before him, he who is a professional army man taught to double his intelligence by promptitude, here sitting before him, he the man whose faultless conduct determined the Marshal to select him out of thousands and thousands of officers, here therefore sitting before him, stark naked and unembarrassed, is the man who in Antonescu's entourage is looked upon as being the evil genius of the camarilla at the Palace, the, king's most potent adviser against the Premier. He sits then; naked and smiles, amused at their encounter, feeling no shame, fact which reminds the solemn officer of a dubious perversion attributed to the king's malignant counselor. Incommoded, he coughs and because he has to say something, if he wants not to appear as being a fool, he asks: "Shall I take you to the shore?..."

In fact, this question contains the embryo of an explicable reasoning for the military expert who by handling the Marshal's secrets has acquired the faculty of feeling the exact pulse of the critical moment he is experiencing: why shouldn't he profit by the situation which has brought the king's adviser into his boat, here in the middle of the lake where nobody can overhear them, and gain his confidence?

The baron, sensing his intention, attacks:

He finds out first about Antonescu's impressions after his inspection of the battlefront. He, as a matter of fact, knows what they are from the account given by General Sanatescu the previous evening, but he exults when the aide tells him that the Marshal was so angry that he wanted to give the entire army a vote of censure. Then he draws him out as to the issues which are to be debated by the Council of Ministers that very morning: the retreat of the army to the Focsani-Namoloasa-Galatzi line, the continuing of resistance in the mountains, the ensuing stages of a possible retreat... And, although he is stark naked, he assumes all his rights of the Marshal of the Royal Household, asking whether Antonescu has set the hour at which he will call at the palace.

With a timid gesture, Davidescu feels as if obliged to excuse his chief: "I don't think he will be able to call at the palace at all; if he is leaving in the afternoon for the Commander in Chief's Headquarters just behind the battle line, I don't know if he'll have the time." Then he attempts to justify the Marshal: "He told me he didn't even have the necessary time to meet Mr Maniu and Mr Bratianu..."

"If he is leaving in the afternoon..." The baron forgets he is naked; he feels like gesticulating vehemently but he restrains himself in time. He feels his mind is blurred. Would it be possible for Antonescu not to call at the palace? Would it be possible for him to evade them?... And as if he objected to this idea, he utters aloud: "That is entirely out of the question; he must by all means call at the palace !..."

The colonel makes a gesture of excuse: that's all he knows, so that's all he can tell him. He draws the boat to the shore, close to where the baron had left his clothes, he assists him to jump out of the boat and, politely, with his irreproachable bearing, he salutes the nakedness of the man who, without being officially appointed, fulfills the duty of Marshal of the Royal Household. Then, dipping his oars correctly into the water, he rows the boat away.

VIII

Ion Mocioni-Stircea pulls his clothes on his wet body and lost in thought while calculating all the probabilities, all the possibilities, all the chances and all the exact data, he heads for the villa housing the Code Service. He is haunted by scores of questions and he would like to concomitantly find scores of solutions. His concentrated look makes the man waiting for him at the entrance to the villa have a sigh of emotion and to tell him with. a sparkling glint in his eyes: "What a fantastic day! Incredible!... First, the Russians' telegram sent to Antonescu; and, now, your telegram sent to the Allies!... What a fantastic day! Quite fantastic!... Yes, there is something up, yes..."

But the baron is no longer listening to his comments. The signal to a state of great alertness is flashing in another sector of his brain and, for the meantime, under the form of a suspicion, he links the present information to that received in the boat. He cuts short the utterings of his interlocutor: "What telegram was sent to Antonescu?!"

Radulescu-Pogoneanu realizes that, carried away with enthusiasm, he has perhaps gone beyond what his condition of a code expert demands - the keeping of secrets. He says stammering: "Well, the telegram... Mrs. Kolontay has announced that Antonescu's objection to the conditions for an armistice has been accepted. Stalin is renouncing the first condition, the one requiring the turning of arms against the Germans, he is willing to sign the armistice with Antonescu without its comprising this provision... The provision will be altered to our advantage to the effect that the Romanian Army will give 15 days to the Germans to retire them troops and will be obliged to turn arms against the Germans only if it is attacked by them..."

On hearing the last words, Mocioni-Stircea rushes off. On the run, he asks where the telegram is. The code man tells him that he gave it to his chief, Grigore Niculescu-Buzesti. The baron's silhouette vanishes into the thicket of the forest...

While starting the car, everything falls into place in his active adventurous mind. The image of the danger is complete: Antonescu is leaving for the Commander in Chief's Headquarters, in the midst of his army and generals where he will take decisions which will be carried into effect long before any information about them ever reaches Bucharest. The fact that his objection to the armistice has been taken into account bears out the report given last night by General Sanatescu after his discussion with the Marshal: the Romanian army resistance positions are still key positions which can hold back the advance of the Red Army for a long time. By going to the Headquarters of the Commander in Chief and by remaining in control of the situation, Antonescu will stop at nothing. The destiny of the country and, also, of the Royal House will take an entirely different course from the one stipulated during the months of preparing the insurrection. There is, evidently, more a variant: the variant of arresting Ion Antonescu at the front. But it entails too many risks and much fewer chances of success...

ANTONESCU MUST BE OBLIGED OR ATTIRED TO COME TO THE PALACE AND BE ARRESTED THERE!...This is the conclusion of this aggressive and combinative character, the fear had the stimulant which cause him to speed the car along the yet empty highway scaring the poultry in the yards of the villages inhabited by the dairy-men and vegetable-growers who supply Bucharest.

The morning sky is clear-blue and golden-hued, shot through by the sun-rays, the foliage of the rotating trees acquires insane transparences while the orchards deeply breathe in the last dewy gusts of the receding late August night. The engine of the baron's expensive car drones smoothly while racing madly back to Bucharest.

....

XI

During this morning, which is heard in its entire clamor through the window open towards the banks of the Dambovita, Mr. Maniu has perused this old-fashioned, withered newspaper which makes many aged people think that their times are not yet over. He has been reading it closely because his sleep, like that of most old people, is brief and not restful, it relaxes the bones more than it does the muscles. Because after a certain age, when the muscles have become inert, that voracious need for sleep in which they recover their vigor, that need for the cozy and restful sleep which is like a rebirth, dies out. Man stretches out his skeleton relaxing his bones which have gone stiff in their vertical position. Gone is the sleep of tumultuous depths, gone is the hot turmoil of babbling energies which flow into the muscles for it becomes as ossified and mineral as the fleshless limbs that it endeavors to restore to life. It is with difficulty that it merges with the torments of the body, but as to emerging therefrom, it does so instantly like the surface mist that is blown away and dispersed by the slightest gust of wind.

And the newspaper found by the bedside in the morning is salvation for sclerotic insomnias.

Mr Maniu has spent the early morning in this manner in his single flat rented on the name of Romulus Pop, in this fastidious block-of-flats located at the south end of Victoria Avenue where another three relatives or friends of his are dwelling.

Corneliu Coposu, his nephew who lives one floor below him and who performs his secretariat work, knocks at the door and enters the room. Two telephone calls have already been received: One from Niculescu-Buzesti who invites him urgently to come and have breakfast with him, which means that not only does he have something to communicate to him but that the matter is somewhat more complicated; the other from General Sanatescu who requires. him to fix the hour and the meeting place for itemizing the matters discussed last night, that is, Mr Maniu thinks, for particularizing the list of the government.

As he is confident he will postpone Sanatescu on this matter too, he does not get precipitated: "Tell him it will be in your office at eleven and ring to Leucutia to come by car and drive me to Buzesti," he concludes. While Coposu descends the stairs, Maniu slips his tie under the hard-starched, white collar made after the pre-war fashion, with rounded corners like the blouses of schoolgirls. -

While he is still buttoning up his shirt under his tie, he is intrigued by another knock at the door. He asks who it is and, irritated by the answer, powders his bottle-nose with quick gestures which he acquired during the time when he was to be commissioned in the imperial hussars. Then he goes to the door and opens it.

In the doorway, with his nondescript expression of quiet respectfulness, stands Eugen Cristescu, the chief of the Marshal's Intelligence Service. When Maniu steps back to make place for him to enter, he notices that an officer in the navy-blue uniform of the Military Court of Justice is accompanying him. Remaining in the middle of the room and continuing to powder his nose, Iuliu Maniu keeps them standing: "Since your visit is unannounced, I must inform you that I haven't much time to spare; I was just on my way out, I have a very important appointment to keep."

Cristescu finds the appropriate polite words to apologize coldly and to introduce the military prosecutor to him and also to inform him in the same breath that he has come to communicate a massage from the Marshal. Then, deferentially, he waits for the powdered head of the sphinx to give a hardly perceptible nod for him to resume his discourse and to inform him on the contents of the message: "Marshal Antonescu, in consequence of your having sent him your opinion on the imminence of the armistice by the medium of Mr Ion Mihalache and Mr Gheorghe Bratianu, has entrusted me to convey to you his willingness to assist you with every means at his disposal, if you decide to take over the Premiership of the State; he will not make any difficulties whatsoever, quite on the contrary, he will execute your orders with soldierly discipline!"

Maniu remains standing in the middle of the room like a question mark frozen to the spot. Staring at the complicated interwoven embroidery of the military prosecutor, he has a moment of sincerity and mumbles: "But why should I of all people take it?!"

Cristescu scrutinizes his face with his highly trans lucid eyes as if wishing to imprint on his mind who knows what important feature of Maniu's countenance and, scarcely opening his lips, he repeats after on old diplomatic technique, the same idea in slightly different words: "Marshal Antonescu offers you the Premiership of the Government and, at the same time, the opportunity for you to conclude the armistice immediately and he asks you to send him your answer through me..."

An answer !... Over the last decades, this has been the most difficult thing to extract from Maniu. His big bulging eyes candidly give one to understand that he does not know the meaning of this word. He puts his lips like a hypocritical old hag who kisses what she most dislikes. Then the aged politician addresses him with his particular false familiarity by dint of which he wants to intimate that he looks upon him as if he were at least his own son: "My dear fellow, this document must be drawn up and signed by an army man!... Only the Marshal can attend to it, believe me!... You must make him understand that, Mr Cristescu, you do, after all, carry such weight with the Marshal!" He insists that the Marshal be the one to conclude the armistice. "We will, of course, support and assist him... And should any problems regarding the responsibility emerge, we will arrive at an agreement among ourselves..."

He stretches out his hand to him as if he was granting him an important gift and he pushes him gently towards the door: "You must excuse me now, my dear fellow, but as I told you before, I have some very important business to see to and I must make haste. And I really do count both on your confidence and on your persuading the Marshal..."

XII

After he hears the door of the lift closing at the ground floor, he powders his face once again and with an agility he has not displayed in public for years, he descends the stairs to Coposu's flat and tells Leucutia who meets him in the doorway: "We shall have breakfast at Barbu Stirbey's... That is at his flat, because at Barbu Stirbey's would mean to have to go as far as... Cairo!..."

He smiles his faded crooked smile and climbs into the car by which this important collaborator of his drives him throughout Bucharest. He asks: "Have they come to your place?"

Starting up the car, Leucutia confirms: "They have been in Sabin Manuila's flat since last night; Patrascanu and someone else. They are waiting."

In a brown study, Maniu looks at the early morning Victoria Avenue along which the car moves swiftly and he nods: "Let them wait. These people, too, have designs on persuading me to take over the Premiership of the cabinet; Antonescu tried it this morning through Cristescu; and the king also aims at it through Sanatescu whom we are going to meet at eleven... Everybody of the Left and of the Right had set their mind on my taking over the leadership of the government, only that!..."

Turning into Stirbey Voda street, their car almost collides with a black car coming from the opposite direction and rushing at the speed of a bolide. Mr Maniu first curses the "damned bolide" and only later comes to realize that it is Stircea's car which has come to a stop and is now hooting loudly before the palace entrance-gate of the royal guard battalion: "Why this is the baron; only he drives at such break-neck speed!"

Leucutia comes out once again into Victoria Avenue and pulls up in front of the Stirbey house where Grigore Niculescu-Buzesti is waiting for them in the front door. Breakfast is only a pretext, and the steam rises from the tea-cups while they remain untouched. Grigore Niculescu-Buzelti waits for the butler to first close the door on the outside and, with a mute gesture, he takes out of his pocket the text of a decoded telegram which he spreads out on the table in front of the leader of his party. Maniu's eyelids shrink while his pupils grow enormously. Owing to the effort he must make to restrain himself or to the excitement that overcomes him, a sound rises from the viscera of the leader of the National Peasant Party and, taking the wrong direction, issues forth through the mouth. He remains silent, with a meditative mien on his face, a genuine sphinx deserving by all means the nickname he has been bearing for so many years. The steam, which rises from the tea-cups up to the height of his stone-like face, appears to be part of the officiating of a certain ritual.

Niculescu-Buzesti guesses by instinct the gravity of the matter so he does not interrupt his silence but stands by, waiting patiently. Many other telegrams sent to Antonescu through diplomatic channels had previously been intercepted by him for Maniu who had then decided on whether they should further be handed to the Marshal or not. But this one is of paramount importance, offering most obvious opportunities for Ion Antonescu to pursue his policy and recognizing him in a way to be still in command of the situation, still a powerful pawn in the future course of the war. The young diplomat, who has been on tenterhooks all this while, gives a start when he sees the lips of the aged statesman open slightly. The parting of the lips takes a long time before it allows Maniu's question to rise from the depths of his throat: "Does anybody else know about the existence of this telegram?"

Niculescu-Buzesti answers him with all the seriousness he is capable of: "The indication you gave me not to let any telegram pass without your deciding on whether it should or not, is law for me!"

Maniu mumbles "All right," with his Transylvanian accent and his withered hands, which have been conducting the political affairs of the country for so many years, fold the slip of paper which he then puts into his pocket. Thereupon he articulates in a more resolved voice: "Well, don't show it to him. We'll see what is to be done about it later. For the moment it will remain with me... Tell me, my dear follow, what did you all do at the Palace last night?"

He is given an account of the incidents and dealings of the meeting held the previous night while the Chairman of the party responds to it either by nodding or by adding something now and again. When he hears that the military representatives, convoked in Columbus Street by Sanatescu, announced that since yesterday all the preparations for the insurrection were ready, he tells Buzesti not to give ground at all demand for the government which is to take over the power on 26 August to comprise only military experts. Military experts alone, there should not be one single civilian minister in the cabinet. And Patrascanu's temporary portfolio, if then isn't any other solution, should be as short as possible, two or three days at most... He wants to add something else but, self-important, the butler enters and announces them that they have just received a second phone call from the Palace which urgently requires to speak to Niculescu-Buzesti - he did not dare disturb the gentlemen for the first call.

Maniu gives another few indications and leaves the house. The breakfast has remained untouched, while the text of the telegram lies safely concealed in his pocket.

XIII

The car of the baron has been abandoned in front of the New House. After having banged its door, he enters the house like a storm. On the corridor he bumps into the non-commissioned officer Bila who is just coming from the room situated in the basement, right under the king's bedroom. He is the king's faithful shadow, his body-guard and the one who charges his guns for him. He sees and notices everything, the baron included, who, even though unofficially, fulfills the function of the Marshal of the Royal Household. He tells him that the king is still sleeping though it stands to reason that at this early hour, 8 o'clock in the morning, it should be so.

Mocioni sends him to wake Ioanitiu and Sanatescu, while he himself heads for the king's bedroom. Silence reigns in the New House. The dining-room and the yellow drawing-room are being tidied up on one side of the corridor while on the other side where the king's office and bedroom are to be found, there is perfect stillness. A footman has posted himself close to the staircase which leads to the rooms upstairs just to be at hand in case of need. Passing through the office where the curtains are. still drawn, the baron enters the king's bedroom and wakes him up.

Judging after the expression on the face of his friend, confidant, mentor, and marshal of his household, Mihai understands that something serious has occurred. He gets out of bed and takes the pains to follow the concise account given to him by his friend: Mocioni-Stircea relates about Antonescu's decision to leave Bucharest that very afternoon, about his intention of not dropping in at the palace and also about the acceptance by the Soviets of the condition made by him regarding the armistice.

The king goes into the bathroom but, since matters require being. commented upon most urgently, he speaks through the open door with the baron who has remained in the bedroom. The footman, prompt in the performance of his duty, enters the room and prepares the king's bath, bathrobes, towels and fine underwear. They do not send him away but in order not to be understood by him, the king and the baron speak English using nicknames instead of the real names. These nicknames had been established by them previously and they were Bij for Ion Antonescu, Bijlet for Mihai Antonescu, the names acquiring thus a certain Anglo-Saxon ring about them; but when used together they re-acquire their local color becoming "Bijbiletii". In this private code of theirs, Iuliu Maniu is Alecu, the same as he is in the messages and telegrams sent abroad, but most frequently he is styled Juanito or Juarez.

In spite of all these funny nicknames, their discussion is extremely serious and precipitated: "Antonescu must be compelled to postpone his departure; whatever the cost!"...

What if the lunatic refuses to come?"

The last words irritate the king tremendously and, with a towel tied round his waist and shaving cream on the face; he undergoes a genuine crisis of personality: "It would be an act of utmost audacity, not the first indeed, but the greatest!... We mustn't allow them to do any such thing!"

The baron makes motions to the effect that he should not manifest his feelings so violently, even though they were expressed in English, because the footman keeps finding jobs to attend to in the king's bedroom. Then demonstratively, with a voice as detached as possible, he draws the king's attention to the fact that the telegram he sent the Allies established the date of the insurrection for 26 August.

The discussion becomes heated, the ideas are blurted and rapped out intertwining with each other, the baron restrains himself as much as possible wishing to appear calm; with lather on his face, the king walks back and forth between the mirror and the door of the bathroom. The footman, who has just been told by the king that he will shave alone, approaches him again. This time Mihai is downright angry because he interrupts them exactly when their discussion has reached its climax. He comes to the doorway of the bathroom and shouts at him: "What do you want, man?!..." The footman does not however lose his presence of mind and anxious to please answers: "To prepare Your Majesty's suit for today..." Applying cream to the skin of his freshly shaven face, the king cuts him short with: "I don't need any suit!"... And while the footman backs out of the room, he lifts his baggy trousers from the floor where he threw them the night before. The very same trousers he wore on his way back from Sinaia and which he also wore yesterday while hunting. The king slips them on and begins to button them up nervously.

After the footman has left the room, Stircea tells him instantly: "The telegram is with Buzel (Niculescu-Buzesti); I left word that they should urgently come over here..." In the meantime the king tucks his shirt into his trousers, lights his cigarette with his lighter and passionately draws the smoke of his cigarette deep into his lungs. They pass into the royal office, continuing their discussion: "Two things must be done immediately - Patrascanu must be informed and the two Antonescus must be determined to come to the palace!"... "We will immediately start to put pressure on Mihai Antonescu. We will force him to make the Marshal come here!... In case they do not come, we shall shoot Mihai Antonescu here on the spot and the Marshal on the front"... "No, that won't do, we must make them come at all costs!... We will arrest them today and have done with it; the insurgents will not shirk from starting the insurrection before the fixed date."

Meanwhile, Mircea Ioanitiu, the king's former schoolmate, his intimate friend and private secretary, has entered the office and has attended the last exchange of views. All three agree on the fact that neither General Sanatescu nor Maniu, nor Bratianu would consent to expediting the action, especially now that the Allies have been announced precisely on the date and hour. Sanatescu - because of his cautiousness and over-conscientiousness, and also because of his definite dislike for all youthful adventures started haphazardly - would be reluctant to take any steps without having first assured himself that everything is prepared from the military point of view; the other two, the old fellows, as Stircea - making no bones about it - calls them now, would be glad to find just another reason to postpone matters once again.

....

Eugen Cristescu, the head of the secret service, makes his own personal plans based on the latest information gathered from sources in the country, from the German secret services and on the results of the diplomatic moves. Secret negotiations are carried on abroad and some members of Antonescu's government try to save their skin by fleeing the country. Piki Vasiliu, minister undersecretary of the police and of the political police department, is about to flee to Portugal, but because of a sentimental affair he delays the flight of the clandestine plane for the following day so that he may take along with him a lady from a rich provincial. family. Facts of everyday life in Bucharest in the morning of August 23, 1944: sports matches, preparations for the trotting race, sentences passed by courts, robberies, suicides, market price-lists, news from the stock-exchange appointments to administrative functions, shows, obituary notices, advertisements, divine services, gossip columns.

Niculescu-Buzesti, director and ad-interim minister in the Foreign Ministry and, also, an important character of the conspiracy at the Royal Palace, notifies the King of Antonescu's armistice negotiations with the Soviets and of their telegram of reply containing the terms of the armistice, sent by Alexandra Kollontay and intercepted by him. Consequently, it is decided that Ion Antonescu should be summoned to the Palace and, in preparation for the meeting, his aide, Mihai Antonescu, is summoned beforehand.

News comes from the front that the German troops try to make the Romanian ones join them on positions of resistance, but despite the Marshal's orders, the Romanians stand up to the Germans' attempts and take on a defensive position versus both the Germans and the Soviets, this proving the independent stand of the Romanian generals who are abreast of the patriotic actions of the Democratic National Front.

The leaders of the Liberal and of the National-Peasant Parties intercede with Antonescu to make him sign the armistice himself, a fact which would relieve them of their obligations to the other parties and to the Palace assumed within the Democratic National Block. George Bratianu is sent by his uncle and Maniu to the Marshal to talk him into signing the armistice. In this way, the political historical parties try to gain an immediate advantage, namely to get rid of obligations within a new government and also to save face in front of history in the event of the country's division or of territorial amputations stipulated by the armistice terms.

In the same time, the representatives of the king try to persuade Iuliu Maniu to take over the chairmanship by the new government.

At them turn, the communist representatives (having not credibility at the Moscow's agents, Patrascanu is surveyed by the more reliable Constantin Agiu), arrives in a secret house in Schitu Magureanu Avenue, where Maniu promised that will meet the left, communists and socialist, for bilateral arrangements concerning the membership of the new government. He is conscious to be the most important and well-known person of the opposition, but don't wanting to assume himself all the responsibilities, looks for a solution to put the responsibility in their charge, conditioning the portfolios with other pretentions, which he will present.

At Snagov, in the session of the Council of Ministers, Antonescu discusses the situation of the front and of Bucharest's defense, while from the Royal Palace he is insistently summoned by the king. He delays a definite answer. Similar pressure is put on Mihai Antonescu.

Eventually, under pressure from all sides, Ion Antonescu notifies George Bratianu of his willingness to sign the armistice with the Soviets, provided that the leaders of the Liberal and Peasant Parties give him an authorization to this effect, specifying their agreement to it. George Bratianu promises that he will bring himself, at 3 hours p.m. the agreement signed and certified by his uncle and Mr. Maniu.

Under the circumstances, Antonescu accepts to answer to the king's insistences and announces his arrival at the Royal Palace after 3 hours p.m.

Therefore, his plan is to call at Palace after all the positions have been clearly expressed and he has come into the possession of the historical parties' written agreement. After that, he is ready to leave for the front to sign the armistice, as results from his negotiations.

In this way, he intends to let the king know about his decision and, before leaving for the front, he also wants to notify Hitler of his decision trough the agency of Clodius with whom he had an appointment for that afternoon.

XXV

The second phone call received from Antonescu at the palace rouses anger: the Marshal has again put off his arrival; he first announced he would come within an hour and now... Until it occurs to somebody that this delaying confirms in effect the certainty of his arrival and therefore the possibility of his being caught and arrested.

The atmosphere is feverish. In the courtyard, under the pretext of routine training, the two platoons of the First Company of the Guard Battalion are drilling under the command of Captain Gheorghe Teodorescu, so as to be able to occupy positions and, together with the five French little tanks, defend the palace in case of need. In the New House, all kinds of reckonings are being made, all sorts of measures are being taken. The moment of choice has passed. Its active, resolute tenseness is entwining into questions; uncertainties and the inherent measures of precaution. The fear of failure, the unnerving desire to succeed, the tension of waiting conditioned by definitely proposed time limits, everything leads to an overexcitement characteristic of such moments. They establish that after having listened to Antonescu's exposition, the king will ask him what he intends to do, then His Majesty will contradict the Marshal asking him to do something entirely different from what he had had in mind. Thereupon he will proceed in such a manner as to bring about the bandying of words between them, fact which should stress clearly the contradiction between them. The king will then put an end to the dialogue and will utter the following words which have been formulated by Niculescu-Buzesti who in diplomacy is Titulescu's disciple: " I entirely disagree with your point of view and therefore I dismiss you from your function!..." After which to Royal Guard commanded by Major Anton Dumitrescu will enter the room and will place Antonescu under arrest.

It is over this last aspect that the participants differ in opinion. Being in a more sentimental turn of mind on account of his former relationships with the Marshal, General Sanatescu asks that the arrest should be as inconspicuous as possible, suggesting that a certain moment Mihai Antonescu should be called into another room and detained there while the marshal should remain confined in the room he will be in at that time. But Mocioni-Stircea and Ioanitiu are together against his proposition. They want the arrest to be carried out in all due form: With a regiment of the Royal Guard, headed by a commanding officer of the Guard Corps who should declare they are both being placed under arrest and who should immobilize them and.so on....

While pleading for a tough and armed intervention, Baron Stircea remembers about his 9 mm caliber pistol which he has from the Polish Count Roman Potocki. He gives it to Ionescu Balaceanu whom he assigns the task to have the car ready to fetch the technicians who are to record the king's proclamation. For any liaison or communication necessities, they will also have two motorcycles standing by, entrusted by the marshal of the Royal Household to First-Sergeant Constantin Spataru and to Sergeant Branescu.

They also establish the positions to be taken up on the ground floor of the New House so as to ensure a most vigilant watch on the yellow drawing-room: Stircea, Aldea, Ioanitiu and Niculescu-Buzesti will stand in the king's office with the door opposite to the yellow drawing-room left ajar. The aide, Colonel Emilian Ionescu will leave the door between the yellow salon and the Venetian dining-room wide open while he himself will hide behind the velvet curtains. And Major Anton Dumitrescu will post himself and three most trustworthy non-commissioned officers - Bila, Cojocaru and Rusu at the head of the staircase leading from the basement to the ground floor.

And this villa which is rather more comfortable than it is sumptuous, built along simple lines with four rooms on the ground floor and another four on the first floor, separated two by two by the wide corridor at the end of which lays the winding staircase, is thus organized in preparation for the arrest of the Marshal Antonescu.

Other details are not gone into due to the lack of time. Twenty-four royal decrees are already being prepared in the office of the marshal of the Royal Household in order to be filled in with the names of all the Secretaries and Undersecretaries of State as soon as the Marshal has been arrested.

Having settled all these matters, Ion Mocioni-Stircea leaves for the conspiratorial house on Armeneasca street where he is to meet Patrascanu or one of his collaborators while the king, beckoning to Bila to follow him, ascends the staircase to the first floor. While climbing, he says loudly with the intention of being heard by the footman and the servants: "I want to put things in order in my stamp collection so as to see what I can send to Peles Castle." But as soon as the first-sergeant, who for several years has become his body-guard, has entered the tiny drawing room opposite his bedroom and has shut the door, the king becomes nervous and excited. He tells him with his unusual accent which his strung-up state renders more stuttering. "Bila, you are my armorer when we go hunting, you have learnt to wait on me at table, now you will learn something new. Memorize this cipher!"

Attentive, with sharp features and a servant instinct, Bila belongs to that category of simple people who have a sure hand and who are very much aware of their purpose in life and whose reasoning has become the logic of a robot and whose one and only vanity is their correctness towards their superiors. Owing to his attentive attitude and his permanently but discreetly alerted senses, the king has come to trust him immensely. Standing in front of a concealed door, the king manipulates six knobs teaching the first-sergeant the cipher, then he hands him the key: "Unlock it!"

A lock of a highly accurate make clicks and the concealed door opens allowing both the king and his body-guard to enter a secret chamber with steel-lined walls and steel shelves built in between the walls of the little drawing-room and of a lavatory on the other side. The shelves are empty. King Carol II used to keep the stamp albums of his famous collection here. But he took the collection with him leaving his son only the key to, this chamber built as if specially to conceal mysteries and conspiracies. Mihai recalls the incident: it was on that oppressive autumn: day of 1940 when Antonescu had forced his father to abdicate... Over the four years since then he had found no use for this chamber. And now its time has come: it will make amends by confining within its secret walls, built by Carol II, the very man, who had compelled him to abdicate. Careful and punctilious, Mihai is now getting it ready to become a prison cell. And since the chamber is entirely empty except for a short library ladder, he sends Bila to find two chairs and a table. He remains alone in the steel-cold cell, the only chamber in this villa characteristic of the tradition of royal palaces, the only one chamber calling to mind the secret entrances, the trap doors, the mysterious passage-ways, the concealed staircases and the labyrinthine corridors.

Since he was a child and he used to play in the mysterious chambers of Peles Castle, he has not experienced such a sensation. And standing here now, in the secret chamber which his father emptied of its stamp collection, he seems to hear the ring of certain royal reports exchanged within the texture of the Palace plots and intrigues in by-gone times. He might believe them; he gives no thought to their literary sources, he gives no thought to the fact that the writers who wrote them were ordinary people. Because now, more than ever before he feels he is indeed the king, meticulously conducting a Palace plot of the nature of those described in books. He will lock up in the secret cell built by his father, the very man who banished his father. As for himself, he had not lost anything. On the contrary, he was the one who succeeded to the throne and that, after his father had removed him, Mihai, from the throne ten years previously.

Yes, indeed, Palace plots which the armorer and royal waiter, First-Sergeant Bila, resolves by bringing a little white table and two chairs which he took from the bathroom next door in order to furnish the chamber for the prisoners of the sovereign.

And the sovereign, dressed in his sports shirt, arranges the table and chairs with his own hands and fetches from a secretaries in the drawing-room paper, envelopes and pencils for he has read in novels that detainees feel the need to write letters. He also sends Bila to fetch two glasses and a thermos-flask to preserve the water cool and to rouse his prisoners from the excitement of having been arrested. He tells him not to fetch an ash-tray as the Bijbiletii do not smoke.

And thus, the non-commissioned officer, selected in the Royal Guard at some time in the past for his height finds out the reason for the chamber having been prepared, he also finds out the nicknames and the pass-word. Making him lock the concealed door and once again verifying his knowledge of the cipher, the king hands him the key.

New everything is alerted; events are precipitated and motorcars carrying messages and important personalities are driving at great speed along the roads.

XXVI

Baron Mocioni-Stircea's car pulls silently along the pavement of the warm and tranquil Armeneasca street. He descends from his car without any haste, he enters a building and rings the bell of one of the flats with the nonchalant air of a man who has been invited to lunch. He is received by the dark-haired man with the distinguished swarthy face whom he met the evening before. Closing the door carefully behind him, the baron, not taking into account his interlocutor's surprise, tells-him: "I need Patrascanu. Announce him that he will have to come to the palace..."

The barrister Torosian, blinks in an oriental manner giving him to understand that he has got the message and that all will be arranged. They agree to meet an hour and a half later.

XXVII

Very close by, in the neighborhood on C.A. Rosetti Street, another car draws up in front of the house with number 37. It is the car by which Gheorghe Bratianu has come from Snagov. He dropped in at his uncle's house on Dorobanti road but did not find him at home. All the family had assembled in the house from where his aunt was to set out on her last journey. In order to bland family mourning with the pressing demands of such an agitated day, he rang up Maniu from the house of Dinu Bratianu, his uncle, and the leader of the National Peasant Party did not object in the least to come and decide the destiny of the dictatorship by the death-bed of the famous Ion C. Bratianu's daughter:

And here they are emerging from the smoke of the incense for the purpose of listening to the account of the developments at Snagov: Antonescu wants a letter signed by them; Mihai Antonescu is waiting at the Presidency for Gheorghe Bratianu to bring it to him at 3 p.m. sharp. Iuliu Maniu exchanges glances with Dinu

Bratianu's tearful eyes: "We'll give it to him; by all means!" they decide while shaking hands with the persons who have come to present their condolences and who tiptoe to the room where the coffin lies. But when Gheorghe Bratianu hastens to ask one of the footmen to fetch some paper and a pen, Maniu tempers him: "We shall give it to him, my dear man, we shall give it to him today... But we have to talk things over first... Look, I for one am going from here to meet Hudita, Lupu and Mihai Popovici. I shall discuss with them, naturally, on the formula for we have decided on the content here. I think you should do the same; this burial is a fortunate moment for a rapid Liberal decision, for I see that all the outstanding members of the party have gathered here... So go and tell the Antonescus that they will receive the letter today; but towards the evening, later"... And he makes his gesture signifying "delay" in the direction of the coffin which connotes an event that can never be protracted.

Dinu Bratianu agrees: they will meet in the evening and they will write the letter: such an important document must be pondered ever for a hour or two... The small of incense and withered flowers cause him to feel generous, so he says to Maniu: "Still, if you want to cheer the Marshal up, you can send him now, at 3 p.m., the telegram from the Russians; thus you would also assist Gheorghe in not going empty-handed to the Marshal... "

Maniu starts as if some monstrous thoughts had been communicated: "How could I do such a thing?! I shall keep and handle the telegram. If we give it to that lunatic, he will negotiate directly with the Russians and not care in the least about us!..." In the other room the choir of priests is heard singing the leitmotif of the death service: "May you rest with the righteous. Oh, God, tire soul of your sleeping slaves..."

XXVIII

A third car...

Tis car which is carrying General Iosif Teodorescu from the session of the Council of Ministers, enters the Filipescu park by the gate of Brincoveanu Castle which is now the Bucharest Military Headquarters.

Descending from the car, the general does not go to his office, but climbs upstairs to the General Staff. There he finds Colonel Damaceanu together with his co-workers, Major Rasoviceanu and Major Viteleanu. He tells them in a flat voice: "The Council of Ministers considers you have drawn up an excellent plan for the defense of the Capital in the event of mass upheavals; The, Marshal has given his approval, so we can proceed to putting it into effect; we will issue orders for the troops standing by to enter Bucharest, that's all. I warmly congratulate you for your work!"

He salutes and leaves the office feigning not to have noticed that the joy of his subordinates is much too great to be due merely to the congratulations he has addressed to them. Much too great, and he knows why!

The three exchange conspiratorial glances. The satisfaction of conspiring and especially their awareness of the fact that they are the only three people who know for whom it has been thought out, what its true goal is, makes them exult. In a few days, the password "Oak-tree, extreme urgency" will became an order.

In a few!... But, today, it is Wednesday, the day which in the Romanian army is dedicated to administrative matters, like those of taking a Turkish bath, of having one's house cleaned and of relaxation. In great joy, they climb into the car driven by Schuster, a naturalized Saxon from Risnov, and they go to the "Brotacei"-pub on the lake's border, "brotacei" meaning in Romanian the green frogs making them noise as fiddlers around the full of glasses and full of company girls banqueting-tables. So prepares the Romanian officer his insurrection!

XXIX

The fourth car...

Driving at great speed, it stops abruptly at the main entrance to the building of the Presidency of the Council of Ministers. Mihai Antonescu, looking like a black beetle in his shining satin suit, descends and rushes up the white marble steps to his office which is on the first floor. Here he asks for the portative typewriter to be brought into the little drawing-room which is adjacent to his office and this having been effected, he closes both doors very carefully requiring that he should not be disturbed under any circumstances whatever. Then he starts typing clumsily by himself. He is typing the paper with a royal warrant which gives him plain power to leave directly for Ankara to sign the armistice with the representatives of the Allied Forces on behalf of a government which he will be nominated by the king, maybe he being the head of. The very moment he learnt during his discussion with Gheorghe Bratianu, that the Marshal was willing to sign the truce, the idea of this inexorable gesture occurred to him, an idea which he kept turning over in his mind all the way from Snagov to Bucharest.

And now typing by himself, secretly, so that nobody might betray him, he is wording this letter hoping that he might manage to make the king sign it. How to persuade the king to sign it had been in fact the food for his thought on his way back from Snagov: he will wait for Gheorghe Bratianu here, he will phone the Marshal at Snagov immediately after the interview with this Professor of history and descendent of the high family Bratianu is over, he will climb into his car and arrive at the palace before the Marshal, in order to spend at least half an hour with the king, exactly the time necessary for Ion Antonescu to be driven from Snagov to Victoria Avenue.

XXX

The fifth car ...

It is Bratianu's car and it is the second one to pull to a stop in the stifling heat of the day in front of the marble steps of the Premiership building. He is directly introduced into the office of Mihai Antonescu who stands smiling and holding his hand over the flap of his left pocket. He does not know the reason and perhaps he does not even notice the gesture itself. But Ica is cheerful: he is reflecting on how, within an hour and a half or two hours, after having seen the Marshal off to the plane which is to take him to Sighisoara for the Dumbraveni High Command of the battlefront and after having reassured him that he is letting the destiny of the country in his, Mihai Antonescu's loyal hands in Bucharest, he too will jump into another plane and fly off to Ankara.

Embarrassed to spoil his collocutor's good humor which is quite visible on his face, Gheorghe Bratianu tells him that he didn't brought the letter as yet but he asks him to assure the Marshal that in the course of the day, before the latter's departure from Bucharest, he will most certainly have it.

Mihai Antonescu lifts up the receiver, speaks to the Marshal ant, to the great surprise of the Professor of history, after having put the receiver back into its cradle he looks even happier. He indeed is, although at the other end of the line, Ion Antonescu has cursed. He has cursed and he has said that if Mr Maniu and Mr Bratianu are postponing him, he in his turn will delay the visit to the Palace, because he only wants to speak to the king after he is in the position to take all decisions himself.

To Gheorghe Bratianu's great astonishment, while he, is telling him to bring the letter as fast as possible, repeating the Marshal's own words, Mihai Antonescu is more and more cheerful.

He is cheerful because the Marshal's ad-hoc decision leaves him alone with the king at the palace offering more chances that his plain power to be signed and, when the Marshal will be in one's way to palace, he will be in one's way to Ankara.

XXXI

The sixth car...

It is in fact the first, for it is Mocioni-Stircea's. He drives it through the gate of the palace and brakes to a halt in front of the New House. He has arrived only after the king and the others have sat down to lunch. They have sat at table just to do something, so that the time might elapse faster, this need to wait is gnawing at their nerves. Imparting to them that he is to see Patrascanu within an hour, the baron takes his seat at table and sits down to eating with a young mans' healthy appetite.

This meal was in fact prepared for Antonescu just in case he would have accepted the invitation. They eat in silence and any attempt at making conversation dies out because they have established all the modalities of arresting the Marshal, they who even contradicted each other on this subject, have come to understand that on inviting the Marshal to lunch they had not thought over how to proceed in the event he had come. Would they have arrested Antonescu before, after or during lunch?...

But they are not in the mood for answering this question so the lunch comes to an end. Following the king's example, they all rise from table and go into his office, vexed by the fact that Iuliu Maniu, who promised to be here at 11 o'clock, is nowhere to be found and that they have received absolutely no news from him.

XXXII

The seventh car...

It is accompanied by the eighth. It is Mihai Antonescu's car followed by his security escort, which enters the courtyard of the palace by the gate opposite the Romanian Athenaeum, crosses the alley which goes around the façade of' the building and comes to a standstill in front of the entrance to the Kretzulescu wing.

The protocol officers having been announced that governmental cars have entered the gate, the New House gets all alerted. Major Anton Danitrescu and the three non-commissioned officers take their positions arm in hand at the top of the staircase leading from the basement with its larders and service rooms, to the ground floor, so that they might keep watch and ward over the whole corridor and the four doors of the rooms on both of its sides. Stircea, Aldea, Niculescu-Buzesti and loanitiu, having made sure that their pistols are armed, open the door of the office to be able to hide behind it. Together with the king, they look out of the window at the portion of the park between the palace and the New House as if to see how their victims enter the nets set by them.

A hardly perceptible metallic sound announces the ears of those familiar to its meaning that the massive door which leads from the palace into the garden has been opened. Then they hear the crunching of foot-falls along the alley, and from the verdure of the park emerge Octav Ulea, the Palace head of Protocol and Emilian Ionescu, the aide on duty, and to their utter astonishment they see that Mihai Antonescu who is carrying his diplomatic briefcase with a self-important air is alone.

From overexcitement and anxiety, the sovereign with creased trousers on, lapses into a state of raging fury. With trembling fingers, he lights a cigarette for himself and makes a slight gesture to Sanatescu. The latter enters the drawing-room where Mihai Antonescu's black-attired silhouette is being projected on the yellow tapestry of the room. The king furiously crushes his cigarette in an ashtray and then crosses the corridor hastily and enters the drawing-room, too.

Touching his pocket containing the paper he himself typed earlier today, Mihai Antonescu is preparing to offer himself to leave for Ankara.

His hand cannot resist the temptation: he produces the letter which endows him with absolute powers to negotiate with the Allies. Holding it out he prepares himself to say: "Your Majesty, through this document I pledge myself to save the country, to..."

But the august rage falls on him with such vehemence that he neither manages to offer his services nor to betray the Marshal: "How is it possible?" shouts the king from the doorway. "What pretexts does your patron invoke now?!"

Still hoping to be able to unfold the sheet of paper, Mihai Antonescu deferentially articulates a sentence which should appear to be as official as possible: "I have been invested with all powers to deal and establish any arrangements with Your Majesty on behalf of the Government and the State, in Marshal Antonescu's place..."

But the king stretches out his arm in an imperative gesture pointing to the telephone: "Call him! Call him up and tell him to come this very moment!... This is outrageous audacity! Tell him to come on the instant!... I am the king of this country and when I demand him to come he shall come!..."

Ica lifts the receiver, dials and asks for the Marshal. Then he informs him of what it is all about in an under-tone as if reluctant to influence him. But at the other end of the line, the Marshal responds vehemently, he utters quite a number of unpleasant nesses about the Palace, where people waste their time while he is going out of his mind with so many problems, the problems of the country... "Haven't you told them that I am busy, that I have so many things to attend to b%;fore I go to the front?" he screams into the receiver.

Mihai Antonescu tries to allay him, or at least that is what he wants to give the impression he is doing. "I have explained the situation but it is not understood and they keep insisting. Look, speak to him yourself!..."

Hearing these last words, and seeing that the wants to hand the receiver over, the king protests brutally: "No, I will only speak to him if he comes over here in person. I have got sick of asking him, of entreating him... Tell him to come here at once!.. ."

Having remained with the receiver clutched in his hand, Mihai Antonescu who still hopes he will get plain power is afraid he has offended the king so he says: "I was referring to

General Sanaitescu. I wouldn't have ever dared express myself in that way had I been referring to Your Majesty"... Upon which he gives Sanatescu the receiver.

The nervous tension has grown to a climax. In their inward selves they all wonder what instinct of self-preservation, what fortunate foreboding makes the Marshal oppose his coming to the palace so much.

Mocioni-Stircea who has appeared in the doorway tells the general: "Don't ask him anymore; order him in the name of His 'Majesty to come!..."

But Sanatescu irritated retaliates: "I know very well how to talk to him!..." And without greeting the Marshal, he starts off directly: "Hello, Ion, old chap, listen to me: you cannot go on like this! Don't you understand that you have offended the king?... And to what purpose?... But as far as I know, you are leaving at six!... Don't say you don't have the time to come!... The hell you don't have time!... I really wonder why you don't understand that you are wrong!... You are pulling the carpet from under your own feet when he, the king, has remained your only supporter!... Well, you see, that's better!"...

While hanging up the receiver, absorbed in what he will have to do, he says: "He's coming! He's coming immediately. He only said that he doesn't like to ride in a car at break-neck speed as others do..."

Mihai Antonescu never thought that the news of the Marshal's arrival at the palace would rouse such joy. He looks, at the king whose face has all of a sudden brightened up and, he bitterly reproaches himself for not having realized till now that the Palace feels such a need for an exchange of opinions with the Marshal.

XXXIII

The ninth car of this race...

It is the car that Maniu has ridden in all day - Leucutia's car. It stops as usual in front of a block-of-flats in Schitu Magureanu Avenue:

Patrascanu and Agiu look out of the window of Sabin Manuila's flat down in the street with interest: is it possible for Iuliu Maniu to have come earlier than he promised?

But is it not Mr. Maniu; it is only his emissary who brings unexpected news: the Chairman of the National Peasant Party is no-longer coming. Mr Gheorghe Bratianu, who has been to Snagov, brought the news that the Marshal is going to an audience to the Palace to meet the king, because he wishes to sign the armistice himself. In view of these conditions, their interview becomes pointless. They will set another date for an interview after they have come to know the details of the new situation...

The messenger leaves. After a few minutes of anger, the two men get down to briefly examining the situation that is emerging: if Antonescu is going to the palace today, then everything is expedited for today; if Antonescu intends to go to the front to sign the armistice, then he might evade them!

XXXIV

The tenth car, and the one that concludes this race...

It is Ion Antonescu's bullet-proof Mercedes... Accompanied by two other escort motorcars, at 4.12 p.m., he stops, before the Kretzulescu entrance of the palace, behind the doors of which the royal aide standing at attention can be seen.

With his cold, malignant elegance, and holding his horsewhip as if it were a scepter, Ion Antonescu casts glances like arrows at the aide asking him what is new at the Palace. The colonel reports in due military form that at the Palace everything is quiet, everything is normal and that His Majesty is expecting him.

Hearing the king being mentioned, the Marshal does not even try to conceal the sever glint in his eyes. And he stumbles over the thick carpet spread out in front of him on the long corridor.

In the New House, First-Sergeant Bila meets him and standing at attention, receives from the Marshal's own hands his belt and diagonal with the case-pistol. Then, while the Marshal enters the yellow drawing-room, he takes his post again at the top of the stairs alongside the other non-commissioned officers who since 3 o'clock have been waiting here under the orders of Major Anton Dumitrescu. The aide, Colonel Emilian Ionescu, after announcing the king of the Marshal's arrival, posts himself silently and stealthily behind the curtain which covers the door between the dining-room and the yellow drawing-room. From where he now stands, he can hear and observe everything that goes on in the salon where the interview is taking place, and he can also see the group of four who are posted on the landing and to whom he can convey his orders by making signs.

Rehearsing to himself the questions and the retorts his followers have formulated for him, the king crosses the corridor and enters the yellow drawing-room. He is very excited. He does not know what gestures he should make. He takes his hands out of the pockets of the wind jacket he has put on over his open necked sports shirt and lets them hang alongside his crumpled trousers. But he doesn't care at all that this appearance makes such a contrast with Antonescu's elegant uniform - yellow top-boots, beige breeches, khaki tunic, all of the smartest shades and hues of color especially if we take into account his reddish-brown hair which is combed in soft waves over his baldness. He does not care in the least and in a choking voice he asks the Marshal to give him an account of the measures he thinks fit to be taken in view of the critical situation on the battlefront.

The question sounds normal and perfectly justified, so the Marshal goes into an ample and detailed account also giving a number of estimates and opinions. He speaks at length, seemingly in order to mollify his anger for having been ultimately compelled to accept the invitation. The king listens to him, he forces himself to listen to him and with the lapse of time his excitement calms down too. He obliges himself to listen and rehearses over and over again in his mind the retorts he is to utter. So that after Ion Antonescu's exposition which lasted over a quarter of an hour, he is prompt in expressing his opinion: "The situation is indeed very bad; you should ask for armistice as soon as possible."

The one who best fathoms the furious but still subdued reactions of the Marshal is Mihai Antonescu. He perceives how the king's boldness to give him advice stirs all the vanities within the Marshal. He sees with his mind's eye how Ion Antonescu's eyes acquire their sternest color, how they shoot arrows, and he hears his rasping voice when he answers very punctiliously that he will not have anyone giving him advice, as he knows very well of his own what measures he has to take. An expression of great concern appears on his face which is framed by his black brilliantine curls. He grows slightly calmer only when he hears the Marshal speak again: "I explained this matter to Sanatescu last night; and today during the session, I made accurate calculations: I can hold out for another year on the Russian front; that means that it lies within my power to reverse the tide of the war. So it is the Russians who should be interested in concluding an armistice with me. This is my deepest conviction, therefore, I will be the one to choose the moment; the moment when I am able to put my conditions !..."

With a passionate look in his grey eyes, with gestures which betray clearly that though the king does not deserve his explanations, he does nonetheless give them to him, Ion Antonescu repeats what he told Sanatescu the evening before and also what he decided during the Council of Ministers today.

While listening to him, his former mate from the cavalry school grows sad. A deep-going sadness has overwhelmed him and is noticeable on his distinguished narrow face. He had made his contribution to the best of his ability to preparing the arrest our of patriotism and the conviction that the country must overthrow the dictatorship. His reason has told him how dangerous Antonescu is and that's why he firmly said last night that the Marshal must be overthrown at all costs. But now, knowing what is in store for him, and seeing Antonescu close by him, still putting on airs, as he invariably does, now when he sees his features again, features that he has come to know so well over the long years of their friendship, he cannot help experiencing contradictory feelings. He wishes everything were over and done with as quickly as possible so that he might be released of his feelings of an honest military man. Sitting in front of them, the king makes believe that he is listening, now and again he retorts in the way that has been planned but due to Antonescu's agitated manner of expounding his strategy, he has only arrived at a third of the pre-established sentences "Your solutions are inacceptable. I require you should conclude an armistice!"

As had been foreseen by the organizers of this scene, Antonescu's pent-up fury is growing progressively. The Marshal does not accept any of Mihai's requests, He questions his capacity of judging or finding solutions for the country; he assures him that he can take care of everything and that in half an hour he will confer with Clodius, Hitler's personal representative, and that he will only take the measures he will think fit to take.

And the explosion takes place: "If you do not accept it would be only fair for you to resign" – says Mihai I triggering off the marshal's furious temper: He to resign?!...

But the king is no longer in the drawing-room; pretexting something about a glass of water or something about his cigarette-holder, he is eager to take refuge behind his supporters who are waiting in his office.

In the yellow-room the Marshal's anger reaches paroxistic heights: He to resign?! How should he resign?! He has a responsibility towards the country; who would ever think that he could leave the country in the hands of a child?!...

His malevolent voice is heard in the other room. As a matter of fact, everything he has said up to now has been heard by the people who have been waiting in the office with the pistols at full cock. They have followed the whole development of the discussion and now they urge the king and they encourage him for the final gesture, just like the coaches do in the intervals between the rounds at the corners of the boxing-ring.

Seeing that their weapons are prepared for combat, the king walks back the corridor at the far end of which he sees the guard commended by Major Anton Dumitrescu, he enters the drawing-room and causes the three men present to rise to their feet – the Marshall, Mihai Antonescu and Sanatescu. He exclaim remaining hard by the door: "Marshal, I don't agree with your decision to continue the war, to my mind the situation is very grave, posing great danger to the very existence of the Romanian people and, from this moment onwards I dismiss you from the function of Premier!"...

In conformity with the indications established previously, on hearing the word "dismissed", Major Anton Dumitrescu makes a sign to the guard group which he heads for the door of the yellow drawing-room. At the same time with him enter also the three non-commissioned officers who articulate jerkily the mandatory salute: "Long live, Your Majesty!"...

But his Majesty is no longer there to receive the salute. As soon as he uttered the last word he left the room by the door closest to him.

The marshal is flabbergasted; Ica Antonescu looks terrified. The short major comes to a halt before them and says: "By high order you are arrested!" In the meantime, First-Sergeant Rusu posts himself behind Ion Antonescu, while Sergeant-Major Cojocaru takes his post behind Mihai Antonescu.

Witnessing the whole scene, General Sanatescu encounters his former friend's awesome look. Antonescu says: "What does all this mean, Sanatescu? I come over here like the honest man I am and you treat me as if I were a bandit?!"... And at the height of his rage he makes the gesture of raising his hand to his pocket, as he always does whenever he is in a passion.

Instead of giving an answer, Sanatescu witnesses with a shudder how the first-sergeant standing behind the Marshal, seeing the motion, reacts promptly and seizes both his hands and immobilizes them at his back. He would like to explain to the first-sergeant that the gesture which with other people might mean the intention of pulling out a gun, had with the Marshal an altogether different significance. It is his gesture of enraged passion: it is the gesture he makes when he is disconcerted and sees no way out.

But it is all in vain or impossible to explain because today, 23 August 1944, at 4.52 p.m., after four years of dictatorship Ion Antonescu can be seen foaming at the mouth and struggling with his arms immobilized at his back by the big hands of the first-sergeant. Foaming, struggling and shouting: "What does all this mean, Sanatescu?!"...

But Sanatescu does not have the moral force to answer him; he. orders the first-sergeant in a low-toned voice: "Take your hands off the Marshal."

A moment of tension ensues: the first-sergeant obeys, Ion Antonescu shakes him off then to sets his tunic in order and is on the point of emerging into the corridor. A moment and all will be shattered - the Marshal will be out in the street, he will summon his guard and will destroy all those who attempted to overthrow him. A moment ...

But the royal guards point their rifles at the Marshal, the group rallies, the king's aide opens the door to the corridor and Major Dumitrescu gives the command for action. With a guard marching in front and three behind they exit with the two Antonescus.

General Aldea, Ioanitiu, Mocioni-Stircea and Niculescu-Buzesti have emerged from the king's office and are now standing in the corridor. On seeing the plotters whom he had long suspected, the Marshal is seized with a fit of passionate noxiousness,

Turning round on the first step of the staircase on to which he has been pushed, he shouts: "You villains!... Tomorrow you will be hanged in the National Theatre Square!..."

He no longer suffers to be pushed, now he climbs the stairs with pride close; on the heels of the distraught Mihai Antonescu. He paces with boldness, uttering abuse and wondering how it is possible for him to be held under arrest by soldiers wearing the uniform of the army he is the Marshal of. Only when they reach the secret door of the steel chamber does he stop with: "What? Marshal Antonescu is to enter this cell?!..."

He offers resistance. He insists on remaining in the tiny dining-room which is the former anteroom of one of Carol II's lewd bedrooms, tire king whom he, Antonescu, forced to abdicate four years ago. And encountering First-Sergeant Bila's eyes and seeing his big hands, he recalls that on entering the palace this afternoon he handed his belt and case-pistol to him, a gesture which made him indignant even then.

He offers resistance. The non-commissioned officers are forced to address him in commanding tones. And it is only Mihai Antonescu's trembling hand which, by clutching at his tunic, succeeds in pulling him inside the steel chamber with a gesture signifying that they have no choice but to obey.

The key is turned in its complicated lock and the knobs of the cipher are turned in the reverse direction. First-Sergeant Bila drops the key into his pocket not aware that it is the only key to the safe that Carol II left to his son.

It is two minutes past five. Major Anton Dumitrescu reports that the order has been executed; then he is sent together with Colonel Emilian Ionescu to the Guard Corps to direct the taking of further action. The king makes for the office of the marshal of the Royal Household in order to sign the prepared documents. On his way he tells Sanatescu whom he sees pacing gloomily: "It's the only solution - you will be the Premier of the Council of Ministers."

XXXV

Ionescu Balaceanu's car draws up in front of number fifteen on Armeneasca street. Mocioni-Stircea climbs out of the car and busy-like, without taking any caution, heads for the door of Torosian's flat. He is impatient for the door to open and when it does, he blurts out: "Have you found him?" Torosian steps aside and the baron notices that in the room-there are several people, journalists working for a newspaper. One of the men from among their midst comes to the door, it is Belu, the liaison whom the baron met the evening before. All three leave the building and emerge into the street where Torosian's car is parked. Getting into Torosian's car, the baron is told to follow them.

At this time of day the main street is empty. It dozes under the weight of the yellow afternoon sun in the family-like atmosphere of a benumbed Bucharest. But for Stircea and Balaceanu, although they are driving along one of the best-known thoroughfares of Bucharest, everything seems to be full of mystery and of the unexpected. Because they who know that the two men who represent the dictatorship are locked up in the chamber-safe and that the country at the present moment is being led by nobody, are driving along one-of the main streets of the Romanian royal Capital, an inert Bucharest which has no idea whatever that the Marshal whose portraits are hanging in all the shop-windows is at present disarmed and placed under arrest.

XXXVI

At five o'clock p.m. sharp, Mr, Constantin-Titel Petrescu appears punctually on Schitu Magureanu street to keep the appointment which Mr Iuliu Maniu has revoked. And he is flabbergasted when he hears from Patrascanu and Agiu about Maniu's latest decision. He seeks to discuss with them what could happen in the event that the Marshal signs an armistice, but the latter seem to have other concerns. He sees that they are preoccupied making certain reckonings he cannot quite grasp

And when the door is opened and instead of the "Sphinx from Bidicini", two of Patrascanu's well-known liaisons appear accompanying baron Mocioni-Stircea, he cannot make out at all what is going on.

But Patrascanu can: he approaches the baron with a questioning took in his eyes. In silence, the latter unfolds and spreads out before him on the table the royal decree with the nomination of the Sanatescu government. And, laconic, he tells them: "You are expected at the palace. The decree appointing you as ministers awaiting you. I am very glad to find Mr. Titel Petrescu here too!"... And he relates briefly how the two Antonescus were arrested.

Glancing at the royal decree, Patrascanu exclaims thoughtfully: "So it is a government of generals after all. That means that Mr Maniu..."

Stircea tries to mollify him: "He was simply nowhere to be found! We haven't the faintest idea where he is hiding. Niculescu Buzesti has been looking for him since noon... And as for you .Mr Patrascanu, you are as we previously established, Minister without a portfolio and temporary Minister of Justice." And then he asks what Mihai told him to communicate them by all means: "His Majesty would like all bloodshed be avoided."

Patrascanu is very stern. Great plans animate him. Nobody knows that the decisions "in the name of his party" or of "the movement" were talked by himself; and nobody knows that he and a few collaborators are replacing by themselves this "movement" formed by people even arrested or emigrated in Russia; nobody knows that the former real socialist thinkers are more inexistent and, also, the little spies-agency which lies now about the importance of them "commando forces" mastered by Bodnaras or, alias engineer Ceausu, is fractured by different interests of some agents or adventurers. But, this one being the reality, he must appear before the other actors very sure of his possibilities and well-convinced, even it maybe only an appearance mimed by him to make them don't hesitate!

Stircea tells Patrascanu once again to come immediately to the Palace, but the latter answers saying that he still has some work to see to and that he will come within an half hour or so, with the decrees prepared to be signed by the king.

After it, he tries to escape by the presence of Constantin Agiu sending him to trigger off the little mechanism which will bring out the first legal manifestos.

XXXVII

Another of the king's messengers, Iorgu Ghica, the Chief Commissioner of the Palace, rings at the door of Corneliu Coposu's flat in the building at the end of Victoria Avenue.

The latter opens the door. When he hears about the events that have taken place, his eyes open wider and wider in astonishment and contrary to the order his uncle gave him, he enters Maniu's room accompanied by Iorgu Ghica.

Maniu fumes: "I am not in for anybody; I am away from Bucharest for everybody!"

Coposu intercedes: "But he is from the Palace!... He confirms what Leucutia was saying. Tell him, Mr Ghica, please tell him."

Keyed-up, Maniu listens to the Palace Chief Commissioner's account regarding the way the two Antonescus were arrested. Maniu, is at first wrought up and then more and more vexed: "I heard the news from Leucutia but I simply couldn't believe it"... he says walking to and fro nervously while musing the young man, the greenhorn, the children at the palace, in their juvenile spirit of adventure, have overthrown all his machinations. And at the very moment when he was on the point of convincing Antonescu to sign the armistice!

With a gesture which has now become futile, he raises his hand to the pocket where he has the telegram he received through Stockholm. And he asks angrily "But what were you relying on, you from the Palace, when you carried out this action?!!"...

Iorgu Ghica gives him the only explanation he himself has heard: "The Palace was w3aited for you from 11 o'clock"... As carver before, Mr Maniu shouts: "This is what the king has been relying on!.. ." And seeing that Iorgu Ghica shrugs his shoulders helplessly, he adds with solemnity: "As I informed you before, Mr Ghica! I am not at home; you haven't seen me you haven't found me at home! And don't come to look for me again, because you really will not find me. I am moving out this very moment"...

XXXVIII

At 5.12 p.m., Colonel Damaceanu, the Chief of the General Staff of the Bucharest Military Headquarters, arrives at the palace late, although he has been searched for assiduously. He is dressed in the same civilian brown striped suit in which he has been at "Brotacei"- "The Green-Frogs-Pub" and, because today, it being Wednesday, the administrative program day for the whole Romanian Army, he figured out he could afford to take it easy in the afternoon, is in high spirits.

The king who was his pupil, and therefore respects him, welcomes him very anxiously: "Is everything ready?" Troubled, Colonel Damaceanu reviews once again the whole situation: he still has to detail the emplacement of several units and also to multiply the order of the Bucharest Military Headquarters. He makes some reckonings to see how long it would take him and then he reports to the king in an encouraging: "Yes, you can count on us, Your Majesty..."

But to Sanatescu when he is alone with him among professional army men he lets fall: "Today of all days, Wednesday! It is the day devoted to personal administrative matters, it will be much more difficult to alert the troops."

But Sanatescu has recovered all his optimism and good humor: "At Marasesti when we defeated them, we were in our underwear; we will defeat them now once again!... Don't you think we will? What did you base yourself on when you told the king that he could count on it being done?"

Although they are both dressed in civilian clothes and bare headed, they each go their way, Sanatescu to the General Staff Headquarters and Damaceanu to the Bucharest Military Headquarters. Not before that the good humor of the general to allude to the smelling of the colonel's clothes: " What a sweet lady perfume uses the green-frogs!"...

Entangled, Damaceanu tries to explain his coming late with the same: "Wednesday, administrative program..." but the General become serious: All is O.K.: you have relaxed; now: let's work rapidly!... I am looking for a plane to dispatch Antonescu to Ankara or Cairo. To not take risks falling the Marshal as prisoner in the Russian's hands! I don't want to allow such a concession to communists. The king promised me, but I want to be sure!

XXXIX

While they leave the palace, Captain Gheorghe Teodorescu appears in the doorway of the Kretzulescu entrance scanning attentively the lawn in front of the palace. Without any definite purpose he looks to be undertaking just one of his routine inspections. Only later, when raising his eyes he seems to notice on the opposite side of the palace square the five cars Mihai and Ion Antonescu had come by, baking in the sun which is shining directly on the facade of the Charles Foundation. The escorts are sweating in the heat. They have come out of the cars in quest of shade. Then, as if out of a friendly impulse, Captain Teodorescu crosses the square and addresses the military police captain Dragoman, whom he knows, inviting him to have a cup of coffee in the palace in the waiting room of the aides-de-camps. The invitation is addressed to everybody. All twenty-five men who escorted the two Antonescus can come, as Captain Teodoreseu promises to let them know in time when the Marshal is leaving. In order to get out of the torrid heat, they accept, take their guns along and enter the palace, saluting the king's aides and the commanding officer of the Guard Corps. The latter smile back formally and when they assure themselves that a platoon of troops has appeared behind them, they ask them politely to surrender their arms, announcing them that they are being placed under arrest.

Five minutes later, a group of soldiers comes out of the palace as if it were preparing to change the guard: and five of the drivers of the palace start the Marshal's cars and turn into Saint Ionica street, entering the backyard of the Guard Battalion. The fashionable worlds continue to doze. The bourgeoisie is taking its siestas. Only the ministers' siesta is disturbed. They are summoned to the palace and invited to come urgently to attend a Council of the Crown, where the Marshal will be present too. They come one by one: General Pantazi, Minister of War, General Piki Vasiliu, Undersecretary at the Ministry of Home Affairs, who, we know, has postponed his secret flight, others... The last, though not invited but having heard that there is a Council of the Crown and who for his personal prestige and name wants to participate, is the Minister of Home Affairs, Dumitru Popescu Codita. Having been received into the palace with all due ceremony, they are disarmed and confined in three different offices.

Everything takes place in an atmosphere of calmness and maximum discreetness. Nobody notices anything, not even when the heavy iron gates opening out towards the Palace Square are closed and bolted and when, on the terrace of the palace, the shooting angles of each of the guns which dominate the square are checked. Heavy machine-guns have been installed at the corner windows, tummy-guns have been located on the staircases and in front of the doors, the tanks are oriented with their guns towards the other gates. Only two entrances have remained open for access, guarded by the royal guard and reinforced by policemen: the back entrance of the Battalion and the small service iron gate facing Kretzulescu church. And in every niche along the corridor a soldier with a shako has been posted.

This morning, Molotov, the Minister of Foreign Affairs of the Soviet Union made a statement in which he reiterated the first statement made on 2 April as to the independence and the territorial integrity of Romania being recognized, adding that the Romanian Army, which is fighting against the Germans for the liberation of the country and North Transylvania, will be considered as a friendly army.

IV. THE TWENTY-FOURTH OF AUGUST AND THE BEGINNINGS

After the king's proclamation broadcasted in 23 of August at 22,12 o'clock, the newspapers publishes it and the "Manifesto of the National Democratic Bloc". The other issues also comprise:

A news item of "The: Number of German Prisoners":

"By yesterday evening (24 August 1944), the number of German disarmed and placed under arrest by our army amounts, within the boundaries of the town alone, to 2,500. Overnight and in the course of the day the columns of prisoners have grown in number but their figure is as yet unknown.

"The number of prisoners captured outside the Capital exceeds the above mentioned figure. According to the operation record books of the military units. Their armament was in part seized by the Patriotic Civil Guards."

Another news item refers to the "Hitler's Bands Defeated in the Provinces Too":

"The Hitler's bands have been defeated in the provincial towns. In the main towns where they tried to put up resistance, civilians joined the Romanian Army units and the Nazis were either captured or killed in record time.

"The rumors launched by Hitler's agents to the effect that numerous German divisions are advancing towards Bucharest have been categorically denied in competent circles.

"If the Germans had any such divisions available they would send them to the battlefront and not to Bucharest.

"Citizens, in pursuance of putting an end to such rumors, unmask the Nazi agents and hand them over to the authorities." One of the commentaries is entitled: "Hitler's Bands Are Defeated! Order Has Been Ensured in the Capital":

"The terror bombing, carried out for 3o hours by the Nazi air force against the Capital, has rendered our radio posts inactive for the time being.

"All kinds of cock-and-bull stories are broadcast by Germans and traitors by means of Ilse 2 and Gustav.

"The Government and the National Democratic Bloc is at work. It is the one and only Government of Romania. Any other news denying this is misleading and foolish.

"The members and supporters of the Antonescu regime are in our hands and have been placed under severe guard. They will have no opportunity to betray Romania a second time.

"This morning, Molotov, the Minister of Foreign Affairs of the Soviet Union made a statement in which he reiterated the first statement made on 2 April as to the independence and the territorial integrity of Romania being recognized, adding that the Romanian Army, which is fighting against the Germans for the liberation of the country and North Transylvania, will be considered as a friendly army,

"The struggle launched by the National Democratic Bloc Government has thus found fully solemn recognition within the international framework.

"Columns of disarmed German soldiers, for the most part former SS troops, can be seen being led under severe guard along the streets of Bucharest to prison camps.

"The combat in the areas surrounding Bucharest, is highly to the advantage of the Romanian troops. Pipera aerodrome, which the Germans were trying furiously to seize, was held valiantly by our soldiers who pushed back and eventually wiped out the invaders.

"Baneasa and Otopeni, where the German resistance was more powerful - and in any case more desperate - were seized by our troops late this morning.

"Antonescu's Guard Battalion fought heroically and proved that it belonged to Romania and not to Antonescu.

"The liberation of the Bucharest-Ploiesti highroad is underway. The Germans are retreating.

"in brief, the situation is good. Each hour and each moment which elapse strengthen the action of the government and the fighting of the Romanian Army.

"At the hour when our newspaper is being issued, the Council of Ministers is in with a view to resolving all the pressing matters of the present."

Another article under the heading "The Army in Full Control of the Entire Country" says:

"Wherever the Germans launched violent attacks against our army throughout the country, they failed to defeat it.

"Our Army is fully in control of the situation."

"The towns Ploiesti, Cimpina, Sibiu and Brasov have been mapped up of Germans.

"The pro-Hitler people have been banished, chased away or taken prisoners. "

The war chronicle comments as follows: "The penetration of the Soviet armies into the Danube plain has brought about an extremely hard situation for Hitler's armies." It goes on to say: "In yesterday's chronicle we stressed the military importance of the overthrow of Antonescu's dictatorial regime and the withdrawal of Romania from the Hitler's war and we pointed out that in this way the right flank of the German combat dispositions has been disorganized there being created a wide breach through which the armies of General Malinowski and General Tolbukhin, are now penetrating into the Danube plain. The penetration of these armies into the area is the first stage of the operation of attacking Nazi Germany from the South-East, therefore from the very sector which Hitler regarded as the toughest. It is most certain that the Soviet generals will serve their combat disposition towards the North-West, in order to push into Central Europe so as to unite their forces with General Konev's armies which are now fighting on the pinks of the Polish Carpathians and along the Silesian road ready to pour into Southern Germany.

"In the Hitler's O.K.W. plan, the Carpathians were considered an insurmountable barrier, but the Nazi generals had overlooked both the possibility of Romania's withdrawal from the war and the fact that the Romanian troops could hold the passes in the Southern Carpathians (from Buzau to Turnu Severin thus facilitating the passing of the Soviet troops into Transylvania and then further on into the Hungarian plains.

"The Soviet advance has increased in the last 24 hours.

"The wiping out of the 14 besieged divisions to the South of Kishinev is drawing to an end. This loss will have a major effect on the Hitler's ranks and it is to be presumed, that in future their resistance will be weaker and weaker. "

A foreign chronicle with the title: "Hitter Has Lost the Balkan Area" reads:

"The German strategic plan for the Southern front collapsed on the afternoon of 23 August. The Hitler's central idea was to hold the front in Moldavia and Bessarabia at all costs, in order to prevent the entrance of the Soviet troops into the Danube plain.

"The reckoning was simple. If the Carpathian-Danube line was lost, the German front instead of being 150 km in length, would be 1,500 km long. Confident in the loyalty of Romania, in April, the Germans brought another 82 units into the country, which coupled with the 23 Romanian divisions, were to hold back any Soviet pressure along the Southern front. On the contrary, owing to the configuration of the relief, they concluded that 2 divisions would suffice to hold back any attempt at invasion. Therefore, in June and July, the Germans withdrew a part of the troops in order to retaliate against the Soviet offensive in Poland. But once the Soviets had also withdrawn a part of their troops, the glance of forces seemed to base been re-established."

Through the overthrow of Antonescu's regime, the Romanian front collapsed. The Danube plain is open. The rear of Hitler's armies in the Balkan area is undefended."

A commentary of the British agencies saying that "The situation of the Germans in the Balkan area is reminiscent of the situation in 1918" is transmitted from London on 26 August 1944:

"The resistance of the German troops in Bucharest has been crushed. The Romanian troops have captured over 4,000 Germans. The Germans themselves admit that their situation in Romania is critical. The new Romanian-Soviet co-operation proves to be more and more efficacious. The German front in Romania is giving way. Over a period of only five days, the Red Army has killed or captured 200,000 enemy troops, 600 tanks and motorized guns. To the South of Kishinev, 12 divisions are besieged, 13,000 Germans have surrendered. Another two Soviet armies coming from different directions have joined forces in the proximity of Galatzi. Owing to the events in Romania, the situation of the Germans in the Balkan area is reminiscent of the situation in1919."

Having entered Bacau, Barlad and Bolgrad, the soviet armored troops have reached without any resistance the Adjud-Tecuci-Reni-Ismail line... The troops of the 2nd Ukrainian Front continue to advance towards Focsani, while the troops of the 3rd Ukrainian Front are making headway towards Galatzi, so as to take positions along the Focsani-Namoloasa-Braila line.

The TASS Agency announces the following news as regards the front:

"The Red Army is 150 km away from Bucharest"

Moscow, 26 August 1944:

"The most advanced columns of the Soviet armies operating in Romania are 150 km away from Bucharest..."

All these news and commentaries certifies that the revolving base plate of Bucharest was working putted into service by a Romanian will and changed the situation on the battlefront as well, maybe, a part of the World War II history.

The commentaries are good and so is the news, a fact which enhances the joy the Bucharest people are experiencing on this day of 26 August when they feel indeed that they are victorious. The Romanian Army has crushed the last strongholds of Hitler's resistance. German Air forces General Gerstenberg is retreating beyond Baneasa, heading for the mountains with the officers and soldiers that have not been taken prisoners.

And thus, on 26 August - Saturday 26 August, the day established far launching the insurrection, the sun rises and floods with its light a free Bucharest, liberated by the fighting of their own military forces. The windows of the houses are wide open in the streets, the sense of freedom is all-pervasive, in the enterprises they are proceeding to the setting up of workers' trade unions, in the meeting-halls, the halls of the long-standing tradition of the democratic movement, ever more legal popular meetings are held, in the buildings out of which the Germans have been evacuated the bases of democratic institutions are established. The town breathes proud and happy for having gained its liberty by arms, by its hands, without other intervention, as will be told after years by the self-claimed "liberators" which occupied us after.

Now, Bucharest celebrates this liberty which asserts itself in its entire bracing splendor.

Nothing can be more delightful, more optimistic, more encouraging than the idea of human existence, than the panorama offered by this town. Only yesterday it was still under the iron heel of the dictatorship, only last night it was still terrorized by the ferocious oppression of fascism which is struggling to maintain its power, it fought arm in hand, it liberated itself and it defended itself vigorously. And today it seems as if it had forgotten all its hardships; all the fierce aspects of its struggle; so eager is it to enjoy the outcome. Because this outcome is called in all its brilliant and life-giving essence: DEMOCRACY...

Entirely devoted to the happiness and pride of having gained this right through struggle, the city has renounced its arms and fully breathes the blessed air of freedom. Only few of the people know that this freedom has come several days earlier, for the insurrection was to be launched only today... It was to be! But it was so thoroughly prepared by the Romanians and paid respect to the Romanian feeling, that, although it was expedited, it was nevertheless victorious.

The freedom it brought in its walked glides with wide-open wings over the town blessing the age-old walled city erected in the midst of the plains. The people are joyful and they feel as if they were all brothers, as if they would like to exchange words with each other.

But exactly at mid-day the sky is invaded by the penetrating roar of bombers.

Everybody becomes alarmed, the threatening monsters cover up the sky again, before radio contact is established with them, their bombs are dropped and explode.

"German attack!...German attack!"... shouts the people.

But they are not Gerstenerg's airplanes.

They are allied bombers which, in conformity with the convention agreed upon, have come on 26 August to support the "launching of the insurrection" in Bucharest.

Like all great armies in history, the Allied air force observes the bureaucratic tradition of carrying out the orders it has been given.

This bombing has as its outcome the fleeing of the last Germans in the Bucharest's neighborhoods, especially the Baneasa forest. But to the indelible glory of military discipline - which executes orders better late than never - the airplanes turnabout left only after they have dispelled a few moments of the satisfaction of the democracy they had come to assist.

Satisfaction fills the hearts of the people.

At, the end of August, Bucharest is experiencing its first day of total freedom and one of those rare days but not unique in the history of Romania. One of those days in which it has demonstrated to Europe that by defending itself it plays a role in the destiny of the entire continent.

King Mihai the first obtained the Stalin's Victoria Order for his contribution to the World War II and, after 60 years, a similar medal from Putin.

EPILOGUE - THE DESTINY OF THE MAIN CHARACTERS OF THIS BOOK

The Marshal Ion Antonescu, Mihai Antonescu, General Piki Vasiliu State Undersecretary, taken over by the commando group improvised by Bodnaras were delivered to the Soviets, prosecuted in the Soviet Union, condemned and executed in Bucharest in 1946.

The mentioned Emil Bodnaras become member of the Politic-bureau of the Communist Party of Romania before to be member of this party, Minister of the Army and Vice Prime minister in the communist's governments.

Lucretiu Patrascanu had a short liberty as Minister of Justice, after it is excluded from the Communist Party and arrested. In 1953 is assassinated in the prison.

General Constantin Sanatescu become the first democratic Prime minister, is changed in confrontations with the powerful Soviet influence, has a galloping cancer and dead.

Eugen Cristescu, chief of the Romanian Intelligence Service, was arrested, prosecuted and condemned to death together with Antonescu but, on the way of the execution's place, he disappeared. It was said that he was at the Russians' demand. His presence was signaled in 1949 in the hospital of the prison Vacaresti.

King Mihai the first obtained the Stalin's Victoria Order for his contribution to the World War II and, after 60 years, a similar medal from Putin. Meanwhile, he abdicated in 1947, spent his exile in England and Switzerland marrying the princess Ana of Denmark, and returned in Romania as private owner of his retrieved fortune.

Mircea Ioanitiu was his secretary in the exile time, Niculescu-Buzesti died young in America, Mocioni-Stircea was arrested by the communists and paid his liberation with blaming declarations concerning Lucretiu Patrascanu.

The colonels Damaceanu and Emilian Ionescu were arrested for a short time; after it, for them collaboration at some historical elucidations concerning the merits of some communists, became reservist generals. Ionescu-Balaceanu and Radulescu-Pogoneanu suffered years of prison, becoming in liberty little clerks. The longest prison suffered Corneliu Coposu, nephew and private secretary of Iuliu Maniu; in 1990 he reestablished the National Peasant party. Together with the generals Vasiliu-Rascanu, Mihail, and Steflea, the colonels Magherescu, Galin, Dumitrescu, Theodorescu, sergeants Rusu, Bila, Cojocaru, all these persons offered interviews to the author

Real martyrs were Iuliu Maniu, Dinu and Gheorghe Bratianu who died in the communist prisons.

Unable to wait to be arrested by the insurgents or condemned by Hitler, his ambassador von Killinger killed oneself in his office from Bucharest under his own picture. Dr. Clodius, whose mission was Ankara, putted in at Bucharest by his own mind, fell prisoner; Gerstemberg and his army, prisoners too; Hansen and Friessner have wrote memories.

Liberated from the Targu Jiu camp by the Patrascanu's decree, the communists former prisoners carouses many days and nights in the house of a priest from Ramnicu Vilcea who became after that the communists' Patriarch; they have arrived in Bucharest only the next week.

The Russian army arrived in Bucharest long time after. In the year 1949, preparing the celebration of the first five years from this event named "The liberation by the glorious Red Army", soviet photographers and cameramen have made tricked photographs and films with worker-troops and happy population welcoming the Soviet liberators. At the other anniversary days these-ones became official documents.

Novels by the same author:

”   Ochiul dracului (The Devil's Eye), Editura pentru Literatura, Bucharest, 1957.
”   Virsta de aur (The Golden Age), Editura pentru Literatura, Bucharest, 1958
”   Puterea (The Power), Editura Eminescu, Bucharest, 1973.
”   Plangerea lui Dracula (Dracula's Complaint), Editura Cartea Romaneasca, Bucharest, 1976.
”   Pretul dragostei, al credintei si al urii (The Price of Love, Faith and Hatred), editura Eminescu, Bucharest, 1978.
”   Patriarhii (The Patriarchs), Editura Cartea Romaneasca, Bucharest, 1979.
”   Insulele (The Islands), Editura Albatros, Bucharest, 1982.
”   Romanul noptii de februarie (The Novel of a Night in February), Editura Militara, Bucharest, 1983.
”   Ranile soldatilor invingatori (The Wounds of the Victorious Soldiers), Cartea Romaneasca, Bucharest, 1984.
”   Romanul unui mare caracter (The Novel of a Great Character), Editura Militara, Bucharest, 1985
”   Faptele de arme ale unor civili; Ocolul razboaielor mondiale sau ce inseamna puterea - trilogie 1986-1989 (The Feats of Arms of Some Civilians" *The Century of World Wars or What Power Means. A Trilogy 1986-1989), Editura Militara, Bucharest, 1986-1989.
”   Poetul ca o floare (The poet like a flower) Ed. Realitatea 1993
”   Drumul spre Damasc (The way to Damascus) Ed. Eminescu 1995
”   Spionii birocrati (The bureaucrat spies) Ed. Eminescu 1997
”   Iarna iubirii (The love's winter), Editura Realitatea 2001
”   Cartea episcopilor cruciati (The book of crusder' bishops), Editura Realitatea 2001

¨ Calaul lui Dracula (Dracula's executioner), Editura Realitatea 2003

¨ "Amintiri din Casa Scriitorilor" - (Remembers from The Writer's House), Editura Realitatea 2003

Table of Contents

Editor's Note 5
I. MADNESS AND PRAGMATISM AT RASTENBURG 7
II. THE TWENTY-SECOND OF AUGUST AND ITS ANTECEDENTS 35
III. THE TWENTY-THIRD OF AUGUST 87
IV. THE TWENTY-FOURTH OF AUGUST AND THE BEGINNINGS 131
EPILOGUE - THE DESTINY OF THE MAIN CHARACTERS OF THIS BOOK . 139
Novels by the same author: 143
Table of Contents 145

www.ingramcontent.com/pod-product-compliance
Lightning Source LLC
Chambersburg PA
CBHW031359040426
42444CB00005B/348